In cooperation with the Pennsylvania Fish and Boat Commission,
Pennsylvania Department of Environmental Protection, and PPL Corporation

Water-Quality Monitoring in Response to Young-of-the-Year Smallmouth Bass (*Micropterus dolomieu*) Mortality in the Susquehanna River and Major Tributaries, Pennsylvania: 2008

Open-File Report 2009-1216

U.S. Department of the Interior
U.S. Geological Survey

Cover:

    Dead young-of-the-year smallmouth bass collected from the Susquehanna River at Shady Nook boat launch near Selinsgrove, Pa. Photographed by J. Chaplin, U.S. Geological Survey, July 2008.

Water-Quality Monitoring in Response to Young-of-the-Year Smallmouth Bass (*Micropterus dolomieu*) Mortality in the Susquehanna River and Major Tributaries, Pennsylvania: 2008

By Jeffrey J. Chaplin, J. Kent Crawford, and Robin A. Brightbill

In cooperation with the Pennsylvania Fish and Boat Commission, Pennsylvania Department of Environmental Protection, and PPL Corporation

Open-File Report 2009-1216

U.S. Department of the Interior
U.S. Geological Survey

U.S. Department of the Interior
KEN SALAZAR, Secretary

U.S. Geological Survey
Suzette M. Kimball, Acting Director

U.S. Geological Survey, Reston, Virginia: 2009
Revised: September, 2013

For more information on the USGS—the Federal source for science about the Earth, its natural and living resources, natural hazards, and the environment, visit http://www.usgs.gov or call 1-888-ASK-USGS

For an overview of USGS information products, including maps, imagery, and publications, visit http://www.usgs.gov/pubprod

To order this and other USGS information products, visit http://store.usgs.gov

Suggested citation:
Chaplin, J.J., Crawford, J.K., and Brightbill, R.A., 2009, Water-quality monitoring in response to young-of-the-year smallmouth bass (*Micropterus dolomieu*) mortality in the Susquehanna River and major tributaries, Pennsylvania—2008: U.S. Geological Survey Open-File Report 2009-1216, 59 p.

Contents

Figures

Tables

Conversion Factors, Abbreviations, and Datums

Multiply	By	To obtain
Length		
inch (in.)	2.54	centimeter (cm)
inch (in.)	25.4	millimeter (mm)
foot (ft)	0.3048	meter (m)
mile (mi)	1.609	kilometer (km)
Area		
square mile (mi^2)	259.0	hectare (ha)
square mile (mi^2)	2.590	square kilometer (km^2)
Volume		
gallon (gal)	3.785	liter (L)
gallon (gal)	0.003785	cubic meter (m^3)
gallon (gal)	3.785	cubic decimeter (dm^3)
Flow rate		
foot per second (ft/s)	0.3048	meter per second (m/s)
cubic foot per second (ft^3/s)	0.02832	cubic meter per second (m^3/s)
million gallons per day (Mgal/d)	0.04381	cubic meter per second (m^3/s)

Temperature in degrees Celsius (°C) may be converted to degrees Fahrenheit (°F) as follows:

°F=(1.8×°C)+32

Temperature in degrees Fahrenheit (°F) may be converted to degrees Celsius (°C) as follows:

°C=(°F-32)/1.8

Vertical coordinate information is referenced to the North American Vertical Datum of 1988 (NAVD 88).

Horizontal coordinate information is referenced to the North American Datum of 1983 (NAD 83).

Altitude, as used in this report, refers to distance above the vertical datum.

Specific conductance is given in microsiemens per centimeter at 25 degrees Celsius (µS/cm at 25°C).

Concentrations of chemical constituents in water are given either in milligrams per liter (mg/L) or micrograms per liter (µg/L).

Concentrations of chemical constituents in streambed sediment are given in grams per kilogram (g/kg)

Water-Quality Monitoring in Response to Young-of-the-Year Smallmouth Bass (*Micropterus dolomieu*) Mortality in the Susquehanna River and Major Tributaries, Pennsylvania: 2008

By Jeffrey J. Chaplin, J. Kent Crawford, and Robin A. Brightbill

Abstract

Mortalities of young-of-the-year (YOY) smallmouth bass (*Micropterus dolomieu*) recently have occurred in the Susquehanna River due to *Flavobacterium columnare*, a bacterium that typically infects stressed fish. Stress factors include but are not limited to elevated water temperature and low dissolved oxygen during times critical for survival and development of smallmouth bass (May 1 through July 31). The infections were first discovered in the Susquehanna River and major tributaries in the summer months of 2005 but also were prevalent in 2007.

The U.S. Geological Survey, Pennsylvania Fish and Boat Commission, Pennsylvania Department of Environmental Protection, and PPL Corporation worked together to monitor dissolved oxygen, water temperature, pH, and specific conductance on a continuous basis at seven locations from May through mid October 2008. In addition, nutrient concentrations, which may affect dissolved-oxygen concentrations, were measured once in water and streambed sediment at 25 locations.

Data from water-quality meters (sondes) deployed as pairs showed daily minimum dissolved-oxygen concentration at YOY smallmouth-bass microhabitats in the Susquehanna River at Clemson Island and the Juniata River at Howe Township Park were significantly lower (p-value < 0.0001) than nearby main-channel habitats. The average daily minimum dissolved-oxygen concentration during the critical period (May 1–July 31) was 1.1 mg/L lower in the Susquehanna River microhabitat and 0.3 mg/L lower in the Juniata River. Daily minimum dissolved-oxygen concentrations were lower than the applicable national criterion (5.0 mg/L) in microhabitat in the Susquehanna River at Clemson Island on 31 days (of 92 days in the critical period) compared to no days in the corresponding main-channel habitat. In the Juniata River, daily minimum dissolved-oxygen concentration in the microhabitat was lower than 5.0 mg/L on 20 days compared to only 5 days in the main-channel habitat. The maximum time periods that dissolved oxygen was less than 5.0 mg/L in microhabitats of the Susquehanna and Juniata Rivers were 8.5 and 5.5 hours, respectively. Dissolved-oxygen concentrations lower than the national criterion generally occurred during nighttime and early-morning hours between midnight and 0800. The lowest instantaneous dissolved-oxygen concentrations measured in microhabitats during the critical period were 3.3 mg/L for the Susquehanna River at Clemson Island (June 11, 2008) and 4.1 mg/L for the Juniata River at Howe Township Park (July 22, 2008).

Comparison of 2008 data to available continuous-monitoring data from 1974 to 1979 in the Susquehanna River at Harrisburg, Pa., indicates the critical period of 2008 had an average daily mean dissolved-oxygen concentration that was 1.1 mg/L lower (p-value < 0.0001) than in the 1970s and an average daily mean water temperature that was 0.8°C warmer (p-value = 0.0056). Streamflow was not significantly different (p-value = 0.0952) between the two time periods indicating that it is not a likely explanation for the differences in water quality.

During the critical period in 2008, dissolved-oxygen concentrations were lower in the Susquehanna River at Harrisburg, Pa., than in the Delaware River at Trenton, N.J., or Allegheny River at Acmetonia near Pittsburgh, Pa. Daily minimum dissolved-oxygen concentrations were below the national criterion of 5.0 mg/L on 6 days during the critical period in the Susquehanna River at Harrisburg compared to no days in the Delaware River at Trenton and the Allegheny River at Acmetonia. Average daily mean water temperature in the Susquehanna River at Harrisburg was 1.8°C warmer than in the Delaware River at Trenton and 3.4°C warmer than in the Allegheny River at Acmetonia. These results indicate that any stress induced by dissolved oxygen or other environmental conditions is likely to be magnified by elevated temperature in the Susquehanna River at Harrisburg compared to the Delaware River at Trenton or the Allegheny River at Acmetonia.

Introduction

The smallmouth bass (*Micropterus dolomieu*) is native to the Great Lakes and Ohio River watersheds but was introduced throughout the United States in the second half of the 19th century (Pennsylvania Fish and Boat Commission, 2009). Today, major drainages to the Chesapeake Bay—including the Potomac and Shenandoah Rivers in Maryland, West Virginia, and Virginia and the Susquehanna River in New York, Pennsylvania, and Maryland—are widely recognized as high-quality smallmouth-bass fisheries with historically strong recruitment. Great public concern over the viability of smallmouth bass and other fish species living in these rivers began in the summer of 2002, when extensive die-offs of primarily adult fish (including smallmouth bass) were documented in the West Virginia part of the South Branch Potomac River (Garman and Orth, 2007). During 2004–06, additional fish kills occurred in the Shenandoah River Basin in Virginia, with 80 percent mortality of adult smallmouth bass and redbreast sunfish along 100 mi of the South Fork Shenandoah River in 2005 (Ripley and others, 2008).

The first documented problems in Pennsylvania were in July 2005, when surveys by the Pennsylvania Fish and Boat Commission (PFBC) found an unusually high number of smallmouth bass in the Susquehanna River (fig. 1) with skin lesions (fig. 2). The lesions were not found on adult fish as in the Shenandoah and Potomac Rivers but instead were limited to young-of-the-year (YOY) smallmouth bass (those hatched in the spring of a given calendar year) in the mainstem of the Susquehanna River, West Branch Susquehanna River, and Juniata River (hereinafter termed "affected reaches"). In addition, no lesions on YOY smallmouth bass were documented by PFBC biologists or reported by fishermen in other large rivers of Pennsylvania like the Delaware or Allegheny (fig. 3). Pathology examinations in 2005 determined the mortalities in affected reaches of the Susquehanna River Basin were caused by *Flavobacterium columnare*, a common soil and water bacterium that causes a secondary infection in stressed fish (Pennsylvania Fish and Boat Commission, 2005). Infection by *F. columnare* is characterized by gill necrosis, grey to white lesions or spots on the body, skin erosion, and fin rot, all occurring in varying degrees of severity (Decostere and others, 1999). Other opportunistic bacteria including *Enterobacter sp.* and *Aeromonas salmonicida* and parasite infections were implicated in die-offs of adult fish in the Shenandoah and Potomac Rivers (Blazer and others, 2006) but not in the Susquehanna River.

After discovering the *F. columnare* infections in affected reaches of the Susquehanna River Basin in 2005, PFBC biologists continued to document the presence or absence of disease in YOY smallmouth bass at sampling sites across Pennsylvania during annual summertime surveys (fig. 3). In 2006, no YOY smallmouth bass captured during the annual surveys were infected by *F. columnare* at any sampling site, including those in affected reaches where diseased fish had first been discovered in 2005. After the 2006 sampling season, it was unknown if the disease in 2005 was a one-time event or if it could be an ongoing problem likely to reoccur. It was also unknown if relatively high streamflows in 2006 compared to 2005 prevented the disease occurrence. In 2007, summertime streamflows were similar to streamflows in 2005, and the disease returned at most sampling stations in the affected reaches but was once again absent from the Delaware or Allegheny River Basins (fig. 3).

During the 2005–07 time period, reconnaissance sampling efforts by PFBC biologists indicated nighttime concentrations of dissolved oxygen in the Susquehanna River near Sunbury, Pa., were below the recommended national criterion for protecting earlylife stages of warm-water fish (5.0 mg/L; U.S. Environmental Protection Agency, 1986). Low dissolved oxygen and elevated water temperatures can elicit a physiological stress response (Ripley and others, 2008) that may predispose YOY smallmouth bass and other fish to infection by *F. columnare* (Durborow and others, 1998). Outbreaks of infection by *F. columnare* generally occur when fish are stressed and water temperatures are greater than 16°C. On the basis of PFBC findings and literature evidence, sub-optimal dissolved oxygen and relatively warm temperatures in habitats of the YOY smallmouth bass were suspected to have played a role in predisposing the fish to the bacterial infections. In most Pennsylvania rivers, summertime dissolved-oxygen concentration, water temperature, and pH follow a sinusoidal pattern characterized by daily minima in the early morning hours (between 0300 and 0700) and daily maxima in late afternoon (between 1400 and 1800). As the sun rises, photosynthesis by periphyton, phytoplankton, and other aquatic macrophytes begins to produce oxygen and consume dissolved carbon dioxide. As oxygen is produced and carbon dioxide is consumed, dissolved-oxygen concentration and pH increase. During nighttime hours, photosynthetic activity stops, but community respiration by aquatic plants and animals (fish and invertebrates) continues and consumes oxygen from the water so nighttime dissolved-oxygen concentrations typically are at their lowest and most stressful levels. Available historical measurements of dissolved oxygen by the U.S. Geological Survey (USGS), the Pennsylvania Department of Environmental Protection (PADEP), and others generally were made during the day and, therefore, represent times when concentrations are least stressful because dissolved oxygen is at or approaching daily maxima. Continuous measurement of dissolved oxygen (30-minute intervals, for example) is the best way to assess whether nighttime concentrations are in stressful ranges that could contribute to smallmouth bass disease and mortality.

Despite the availability of continuous water-quality data at some locations in the Susquehanna River, substantial data gaps exist. Recognizing the need for additional information, the USGS in cooperation with the PFBC, the PADEP, and PPL Corporation (PPL), conducted a study from May through October 2008 to assess water quality in selected reaches of the Susquehanna River and major tributaries where mortalities of smallmouth bass were documented. The results of the study are presented in this report. The data and interpretations within this report document conditions in 2008 and could be used as a foundation for development of a long-term network of data collection and interpretation.

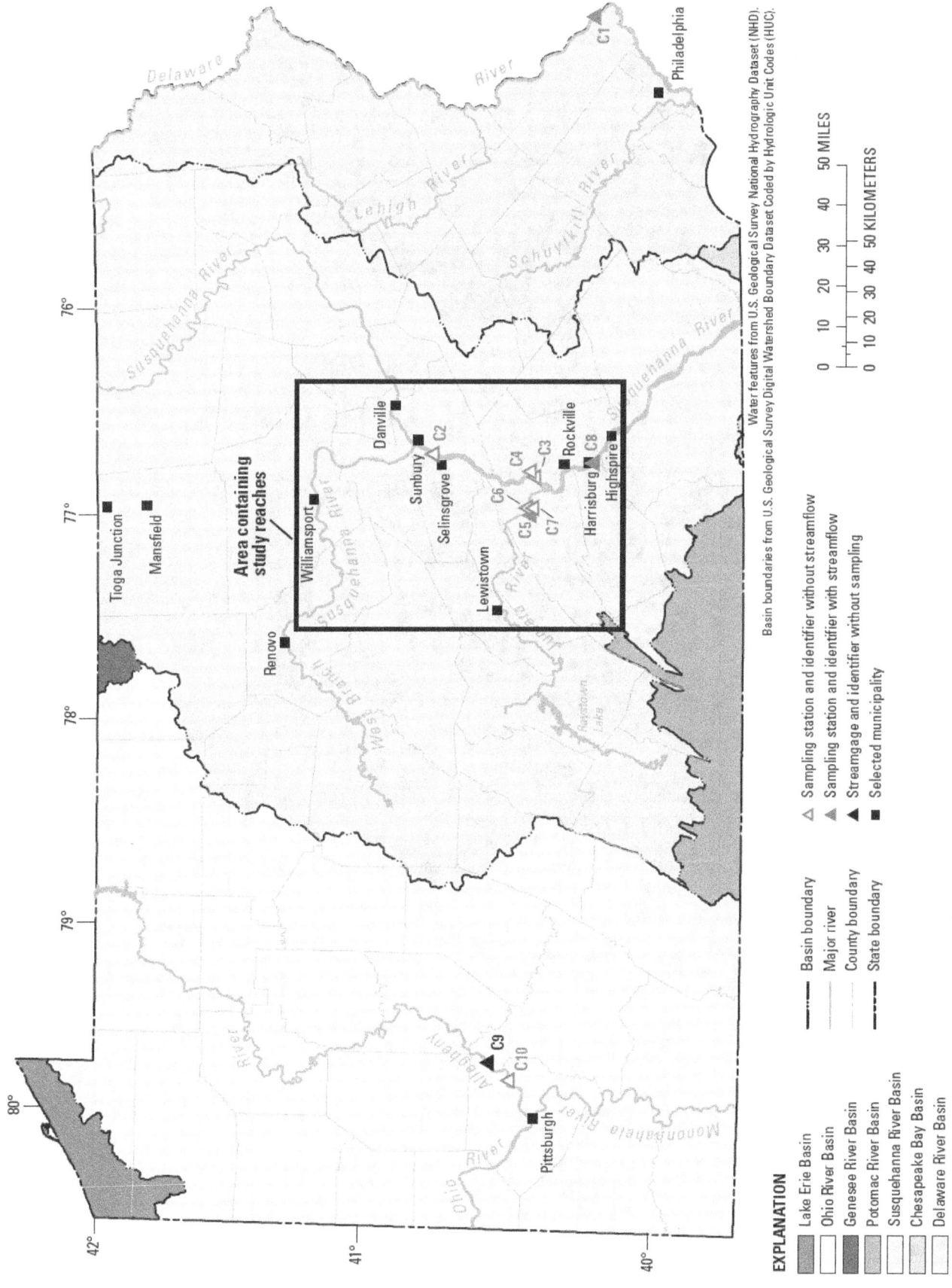

Figure 1. Location of selected continuous water-quality monitoring stations in the Delaware, Susquehanna, and Ohio River Basins, Pennsylvania, 2008.

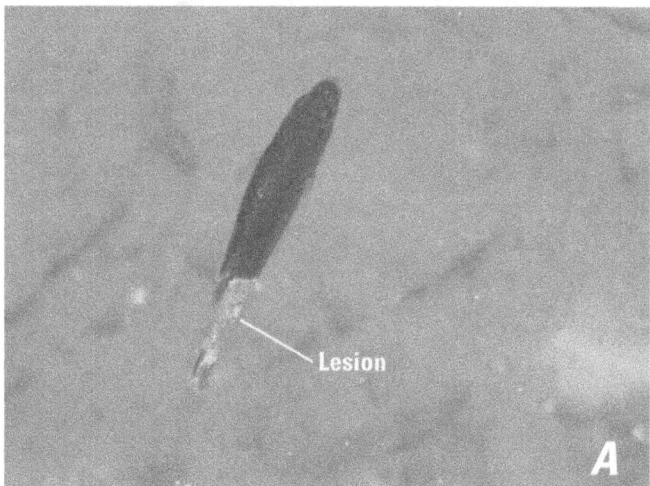

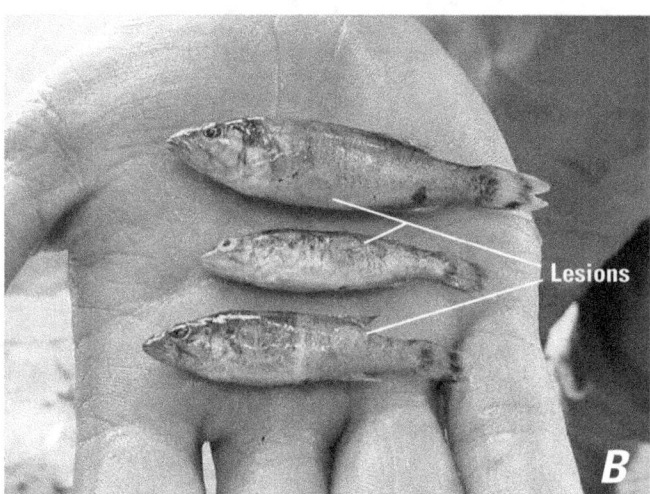

Figure 2.   Moribund (*A*) and dead (*B*) young-of-the-year smallmouth bass (*Micropterus dolomieu*) with skin lesions caused by *Flavobacterium columnare* bacteria. (The fish are approximately 2 inches long. Photograph *A* by Jeffrey Chaplin, U.S. Geological Survey, July 14, 2008; Photograph *B* by Pennsylvania Fish and Boat Commission).

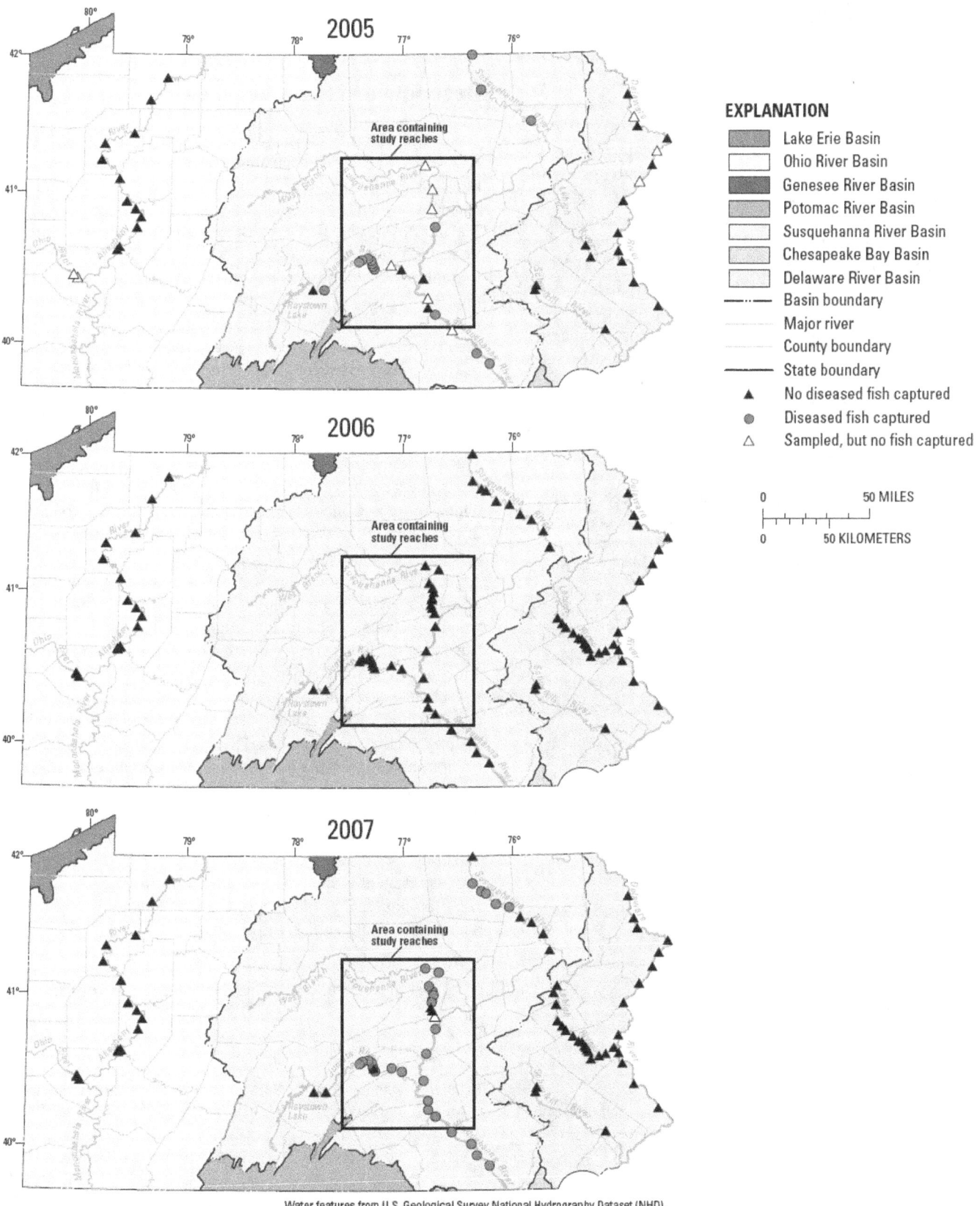

Figure 3.   Geographic distribution of disease incidence in young-of-the-year smallmouth bass, Pennsylvania, 2005–07.

Purpose and Scope

This report presents results and analysis of water-quality data collected from seven continuous (30-minute interval) water-quality meters (sondes) measuring dissolved oxygen, temperature, pH, and specific conductance. It also provides streamflow data from the Delaware, Susquehanna, Juniata, and Allegheny Rivers for the 2008 water year[1]. Water quality of main-channel habitat and YOY smallmouth-bass microhabitat on the Susquehanna and Juniata Rivers is compared using data from four sondes that were deployed as pairs. For the purpose of this report, microhabitat is defined as habitat where YOY smallmouth bass spend the first 2–3 months of their lives and is characterized by backwater and shoreline areas with relatively low velocities and depths compared to the main channel.

Two additional sondes were collocated with streamgages at Harrisburg and Newport, Pa. Historical streamflow and water-quality conditions in the Susquehanna River at Harrisburg, Pa., are compared with water-quality and streamflow data collected in 2008 at Harrisburg, Pa. The seventh sonde was deployed in July 2008 in the Susquehanna River near Selinsgrove, Pa., a location where bacterial infections were discovered during the 2008 annual surveys for YOY smallmouth bass by PFBC fisheries biologists (Robert Lorantas, Pennsylvania Fish and Boat Commission, written commun., 2008). The report also examines water-quality differences between the Susquehanna River where YOY smallmouth-bass mortalities have occurred and the Delaware and Allegheny Rivers where no mortalities have been documented. The purpose of this comparison is to determine if water-quality conditions in the Susquehanna River are more stressful than in the Delaware or Allegheny Rivers.

Finally, concentrations of nitrogen and phosphorus in water and streambed-sediment samples along with biochemical oxygen demand (BOD) in water collected at 25 locations in the Susquehanna River and tributaries between Williamsport and Highspire, Pa., on June 11 and 12, 2008, are presented. Nutrient concentrations in the Susquehanna River

Basin are compared with concentrations reported to promote growth of algae and other aquatic vegetation.

Description of Study Reaches

The Susquehanna River flows generally southward for about 447 mi from its headwaters near Cooperstown, N.Y., to the Chesapeake Bay in Maryland. The river drains 20,962 mi[2] of Pennsylvania (fig. 1) including parts of the Appalachian Plateau Physiographic Province in northern and west-central Pennsylvania and the Ridge and Valley and Piedmont Physiographic Provinces in central and south-central Pennsylvania (Pennsylvania Department of Conservation and Natural Resources, 2000). The West Branch Susquehanna River enters the mainstem between Danville and Sunbury, Pa. Streamflow records from 1951 through 1980 indicate that the mainstem upstream of the West Branch contributes about 40 percent of the streamflow measured at Conowingo, Md., before the Susquehanna River flows into the Chesapeake Bay, and the West Branch contributes about 28 percent. The Juniata River contributes about 11 percent of the streamflow in the Susquehanna River at Conowingo, Md., and is the largest tributary downstream of the West Branch. Historical streamflows for selected stations are summarized in table 1.

The study reaches that were selected to represent the affected reaches in the basin include the Susquehanna River roughly between Danville and Highspire, Pa., the West Branch Susquehanna River from Williamsport to the mouth, and the Juniata River from Lewistown, Pa., to the mouth (fig. 1). Established continuous water-quality stations in the Delaware and Allegheny River Basins were used for comparison with stations on the study reaches. The study reaches are underlain predominantly by shale and sandstone (Cuff and others, 1989); some upstream reaches and tributary streams flow through areas underlain by strata containing anthracite and bituminous coal. Bedrock is close to the land surface and is a common substrate for the Susquehanna River streambed. Because bedrock is resistant to the erosional forces of flowing water, the free-flowing reaches of the Susquehanna River tend to be wide and shallow compared to most other rivers.

---

[1]Water year is defined as the year beginning on October 1 and ending September 30.

Table 1.   Summary statistics for historical streamflow at selected streamgages in study reaches of the Susquehanna River Basin, Pennsylvania.

[mi², square miles; ft³/s, cubic feet per second; WY, water year beginning on October 1 and ending September 30]

Streamgage	Period of record	Drainage area (mi²)	Annual mean streamflow (ft³/s)[1]	Highest annual mean streamflow (ft³/s)[1]	Lowest annual mean streamflow (ft³/s)[1]
Susquehanna River at Danville	Mar. 1899 to Present	11,220	17,680	24,670 in WY 1978	6,948 in WY 1965
West Branch Susquehanna River at Lewisburg	Oct. 1939 to Present	6,847	10,600	17,760 in WY 2004	6,158 in WY 1965
Susquehanna River at Sunbury	Oct. 1937 to Present	18,300	27,131	43,380 in WY 2004	13,420 in WY 1965
Juniata River at Newport	Apr. 1899 to Present	3,354	4,505	7,470 in WY 2004	2,241 in WY 2002

[1]For period of record ending September 30, 2007.

Dissolved-Oxygen Criteria and Standards for Protection of Aquatic Life

The solubility of oxygen in equilibrium with water and air is inversely correlated with water temperature (fig. 4) but positively correlated with atmospheric pressure. As a result, dissolved-oxygen concentrations are greater for conditions characterized by cold water and high atmospheric pressure than for warm water and low atmospheric pressure. In summertime and early fall, equilibrium conditions rarely are achieved because of photosynthesis and respiration. During the day, the rate of oxygen production by photosynthesis exceeds the rate that oxygen exsolves into the atmosphere. As a result, the water becomes supersaturated with oxygen despite relatively high daytime water temperatures. By contrast, cooler nighttime water temperature generally are accompanied by lower dissolved-oxygen concentrations because respiration consumes oxygen in the water faster than it dissolves into the water column.

Water that is undersaturated will entrain oxygen from the atmosphere, a process referred to as reaeration. Turbulence enhances reaeration. Therefore, the rate of reaeration is slower in slow-moving microhabitats compared to the more turbulent and faster-moving water in the main channel of a river. Thus, different dissolved-oxygen concentrations would be expected in YOY smallmouth-bass microhabitats compared to main-channel habitats because of the effects of reaeration alone.

Because of continued oxygen consumption by respiration and the cessation of photosynthesis at night, low oxygen levels can result in and have been shown to cause lethal and sub-lethal physiological and behavioral effects in many organisms, especially fish (Welker and others, 2007; Canadian Council of Ministers of the Environment, 1999; U.S. Environmental Protection Agency, 1986; Spoor, 1984; Siefert and others, 1974). Earlylife stages are more sensitive to exposure to low dissolved-oxygen concentrations than adult fish (U.S.

Environmental Protection Agency, 1986), and these sensitivities commonly are magnified at higher temperatures (Spoor, 1984). For example, smallmouth-bass larvae, which are highly sensitive to oxygen deficiency between the second and tenth days after hatching, were exposed to a sustained dissolved-oxygen concentration of 4.0 mg/L and temperatures of 20°C and 25°C in an experiment described in Spoor (1984). The normally sluggish larvae exhibited increased behavioral response at 25°C compared to 20°C, including swimming to the surface.

Because the response to low dissolved-oxygen concentrations varies with life stage, the U.S. Environmental Protection Agency (EPA) has recommended national dissolved-oxygen criteria for protecting earlylife stages and other life stages for non-salmonid warm-water species, including smallmouth bass (table 2). Criteria for dissolved-oxygen concentrations established in 1986 were based on available results primarily from laboratory tests conducted at temperatures near the mid-range of a species temperature tolerance. Thus, recommended criteria that are based on these laboratory tests may be under-protective at higher temperatures and over-protective at lower temperatures (U.S. Environmental Protection Agency, 1986). For the purpose of this report, stressful conditions are considered to exist when the dissolved-oxygen concentration is at or below the applicable criteria recommended by the U.S. Environmental Protection Agency (1986).

Although EPA has recommended criteria for dissolved oxygen, PADEP has adopted standards that are applicable on a statewide basis (Pennsylvania Department of Environmental Protection, 2009a). These PADEP standards are somewhat less protective (lower) than the national criteria (table 3).

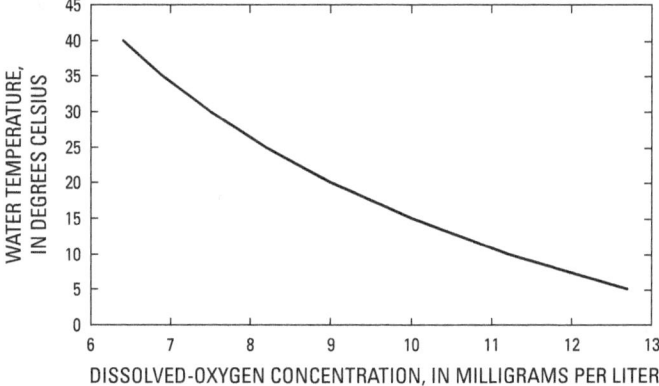

Figure 4. Solubility of oxygen in water at temperatures ranging from 5 to 40 degrees Celsius and atmospheric pressure of 755 millimeters of mercury. [Data for graph compiled from Wilde and others (1998)]

Table 2. National criteria for ambient dissolved-oxygen concentrations for protection of warm-water fishes.

[Criteria recommended by U.S. Environmental Protection Agency, 1986; NA, not applicable; 30-day mean, mean of daily means measured over a 30-day period; 7-day mean; mean of daily means measured over a 7-day period; 7-day mean minimum, mean of daily minimum values measured over a 7-day period; Instantaneous minimum, minimum value measured on any given day]

Statistic	Warm-water criteria, in milligrams per liter	
	Earlylife stages[1]	Other life stages
30-day mean	NA	5.5
7-day mean	6.0	NA
7-day mean minimum	NA	4.0
Instantaneous minimum	5.0	3.0

[1]Includes all embryonic and larval stages and all juvenile forms to 30 days following hatching.

Table 3. Pennsylvania standards for dissolved-oxygen concentration in waters designated as warm-water fisheries.

[Minimum daily mean, minimum arithmetic average of samples collected during a continuous 24-hour period]

Statistic	Warm-water standards for all life stages, in milligrams per liter
Minimum daily mean	5.0
Instantaneous minimum	4.0

Monitoring Strategy

Spawning behavior of smallmouth bass, data from YOY smallmouth-bass surveys, and reconnaissance efforts by PFBC biologists indicating low dissolved-oxygen concentrations were all used to develop the monitoring strategy for this study. Further, the low flows and warm temperatures when the bacterial infections were observed in 2005 and 2007, compared to the higher flows and cooler temperatures when bacterial infections were not observed in 2006, suggested an underlying environmental cause for the problem.

Adult and YOY smallmouth-bass surveys by PFBC biologists indicate that YOY smallmouth bass in affected reaches of the Susquehanna River were being infected by *F. columnare* usually in July, but adult smallmouth bass and other species of fish that died during fish kills in the Potomac River mostly were not infected with *F. columnare* (Pennsylvania Fish and Boat Commission, 2005). Because YOY smallmouth bass were primarily affected in the Susquehanna River, spawning behavior and nest-site selection were evaluated to develop a strategy for where and over what time period to monitor water quality.

In the Susquehanna River Basin, smallmouth bass typically spawn from late April to early June, when water temperature reaches approximately 15°C. Males sweep out a nest site in gravel or sand-sized substrate with their caudal fin and court females to deposit eggs in the nest, a process that can take hours to weeks. Nests typically are constructed in microhabitats characterized by relatively low velocities and depths of at least 0.8 ft (Dauwalter and Fisher, 2007). After the eggs are deposited and fertilized, males guard the nest while the embryos develop and provide sole parental care of the offspring (Ridgway and others, 1989). Depending on water temperature, the eggs hatch in 2 to 9 days and the young fish are ready to leave the nest (commonly referred to as swim up) and disperse in 5 to 6 days. The newly hatched fish are susceptible to predation and cannot withstand velocities common to main-channel habitats. As a result, the first 2 to 3 months after swim up (roughly May through July) are spent in the same microhabitat where they were born. During this time, YOY smallmouth bass require greater dissolved-oxygen concentrations for proper development and survival (U.S. Environmental Protection Agency, 1986). For the purpose of this report,

the timeframe of May 1 through July 31 will be referred to as the critical period.

Because YOY smallmouth bass live in different habitats than adult fish, they may be exposed to different dissolved-oxygen concentrations and temperatures. This may be caused by varying exposure to sunlight and abundance of plant life, different reaeration rates, or different levels of sediment-oxygen demand. Microhabitats where YOY smallmouth bass live and main-channel habitats where adults primarily live were compared by deploying paired sondes with one in YOY smallmouth-bass microhabitat and another in nearby faster-moving waters of the main part of the channel. These paired sondes are differentiated as "microhabitat" and "main-channel" throughout this report. If low dissolved-oxygen concentrations and (or) high temperatures exist, they may stress and predispose YOY smallmouth bass to infection by the bacteria. Because YOY smallmouth bass in the Susquehanna River Basin were infected by *F. columnare* but fish in the Delaware and the Allegheny River Basins were not, sondes deployed in main-channel habitats of the Delaware and Allegheny Rivers were used for comparison with conditions in main-channel habitat of the Susquehanna River.

Study Design

F. columnare is widely recognized by the aquaculture industry and others as a dangerous pathogen to catfish, tilapia, and other fish reared in crowded conditions (Durborow and others, 1998; Suomalainen and others, 2005), but the bacteria typically does not infect unstressed smallmouth bass in riverine systems (Noga, 1988). Capture rates of YOY smallmouth bass by PFBC biologists from 1987 to 2008 (Robert Lorantas, Pennsylvania Fish and Boat Commission, written commun., 2009) indicate crowding is not likely to stress or otherwise predispose these fish to infection (John Arway, Pennsylvania Fish and Boat Commission, oral commun., 2009). However, other environmental stressors that may predispose fish to colonization by *F. columnare* include low dissolved oxygen, elevated ammonia, elevated nitrite, and warm water temperatures (Durborow and others, 1998). Low dissolved oxygen and (or) elevated water temperatures, along with other environmental stressors, have the potential to cause a physiological stress response, resulting in altered circulating concentrations of the hormone cortisol (Ripley and others, 2008). Immunosuppression is a well-characterized effect of increased cortisol concentrations, causing reductions in circulating immune cell numbers and bactericidal activity coinciding with an inflammatory response (Maule and Schreck, 1990; Wang and others, 2005). The working hypothesis for this study is that dissolved-oxygen concentrations and water temperatures in study reaches of the Susquehanna River are at times stressful to YOY smallmouth bass. Stress induced by low dissolved-oxygen concentrations, high water temperatures, and other environmental factors may immunosuppress YOY smallmouth bass and thereby predispose them to infection by *F. columnare*.

The study was designed to document environmental conditions during the critical period for YOY smallmouth bass to determine whether stressful water-quality conditions occurred in microhabitats and main-channel habitats in 2008. Furthermore, the study attempted to document whether environmental conditions were different in smallmouth-bass microhabitats compared to main-channel locations. If so, this could be a factor explaining why YOY fish are affected whereas adults are not. Stations recording water-quality constituents on a continuous basis (referred to hereinafter as "continuous-monitoring stations") and stations where nutrient samples were collected (referred to hereinafter as "nutrient synoptic stations") (table 4) were located in reaches where mortalities of smallmouth bass were documented in 2005 and 2007 (fig. 3). Finally, because diseased YOY smallmouth bass were observed in the Susquehanna River but not in the Delaware or Allegheny Rivers, comparisons of water-quality conditions among these rivers were planned as part of the study design.

Monitoring Stations

Cross-section geometry and flow characteristics vary greatly among the sites where the monitoring stations (including the continuous-monitoring stations and the nutrient synoptic stations) are located. For example, the width-to-mean-depth ratio in riffle cross sections in the Susquehanna River at Clemson Island (fig. 5B) is 1,853 ft/ft compared to 392 ft/ft for the Delaware River at Trenton (fig. 5A). Because the Susquehanna River at this site has a large width relative to its depth, the surface area exposed to sunlight is large, which results in relatively quick warming and cooling in comparison to the narrower Delaware River at Trenton. The river cross sections containing each sonde are described in more detail below, including the cross sections at stations in the Delaware and Allegheny Rivers. For the purpose of comparison among cross sections, river depths shown in figs. 5 and 6 are normalized to streamflow conditions on June 23, 2008, at 1600 hrs, a time of base flow.

Susquehanna River at Shady Nook Boat Launch

Although no channel cross-section data from streamflow measurements or other surveys were available at this cross section, the channel here is morphologically similar to most other affected reaches of the Susquehanna River. The cross section is characterized by pool habitat split into two primary channels by a large island in the middle. Total river width, including the island, is about 3,000 ft at base-flow conditions. The larger of the two primary channels is about 1,100 ft wide and is on the right side of the island. Throughout this report, the terms "right bank," "left bank," "right side," and "left side" are determined while looking downstream and are used to identify the sampling locations and channel features.

On July 14, 2008, annual YOY smallmouth-bass surveys by PFBC biologists found *F. columnare* infections near the

Shady Nook boat launch (near Selinsgrove, Pa.). In response to this finding, a sonde was deployed on July 16, 2008, at station C2 (Susquehanna River at Shady Nook Boat Launch) about 15 ft from the right bank of the right channel in flowing water of moderate velocity. There was no backwater effect from channel bars or other upstream features that divert or alter streamflow; however, abundant rooted aquatic plants were growing in the right channel in the vicinity of the sonde. A coal-fired power plant about 1.27 mi upstream from this station withdraws river water for cooling and discharges the heated effluent into the channel.

Susquehanna River in the Vicinity of Clemson Island

The Susquehanna River at Clemson Island includes riffle and pool habitat. The width of the channel at the cross section in figure 5B is more than six times wider than comparable habitat monitored in the Juniata River, but the depth is only slightly greater (figs. 5B and D). The width during base-flow conditions is about 3,630 ft, and maximum depth estimated for base-flow conditions on June 23, 2008, was 4.5 ft. This cross section has three channels, but the right channel carries the majority of streamflow. The microhabitat sonde was deployed at station C4 on May 16, 2008 (Susquehanna River at Clemson Island [Microhabitat]), in a backwater eddy off the east shore of Clemson Island where water was less than 2 ft deep during summer base flow. The main-channel sonde was deployed at station C3 (Susquehanna River below Clemson Island [Main Channel]) about 850 ft downstream of the microhabitat sonde and 25 ft streamward of the west shore of a small linear island downstream from Clemson Island (fig. 5B). Water depth at the main-channel sonde was comparable to depths in the microhabitat, but the water velocity was appreciably greater.

Juniata River at Newport, Pennsylvania

The channel cross section of the Juniata River at Newport, Pa., was characterized from width and depth data collected during a bridge measurement made from the S.R. 34 Bridge in November 2007. The channel at this cross section is predominantly pool habitat and has a width of about 550 ft under base-flow conditions (fig. 5C). The maximum depth estimated for base-flow conditions on June 23, 2008, was 6.8 ft. The sonde was deployed on May 8, 2008, at station C5 (Juniata River at Newport, Pa.) in main-channel habitat about 20 ft from the right bank. The water was about 2.5 ft deep during normal base-flow conditions. Velocity data from the measurement in November 2007 indicate velocities in the vicinity of the sonde are greater than the average velocity in the cross section (1.39 to 1.79 ft/s in the vicinity of the sonde, compared to an average of 1.33 ft/s for the cross section).

Table 4. Stations for collection of streamflow, continuous water-quality data, and nutrient synoptic samples, Pennsylvania, 2008.

[mi², square miles]

Station number	Map identifier	Station description	Drainage area (mi²)	Latitude	Longitude
		Continuous Data Stations			
01463500	C1	Delaware River at Trenton, N.J.	6,780	40° 13' 18.0"	74° 46' 41.0"
01554010	C2	Susquehanna River at Shady Nook Boat Launch	18,432	40° 49' 21.5"	76° 50' 21.9"
[1]01555710	C3	Susquehanna River below Clemson Island (Main Channel)	19,673	40° 27' 42.1"	76° 56' 56.1"
01555725	C4	Susquehanna River at Clemson Island (Microhabitat)	19,674	40° 27' 47.8"	76° 56' 46.3"
[1]01567000	C5	Juniata River at Newport, Pa.	3,354	[2]40° 28' 42.0"	[2]77° 07' 46.0"
01567150	C6	Juniata River near Howe Township Park (Microhabitat)	3,379	40° 29' 29.2"	77° 05' 52.5"
01567151	C7	Juniata River near Howe Township Park (Main Channel)	3,379	40° 29' 28.2"	77° 05' 50.8"
[1]01570500	C8	Susquehanna River at Harrisburg, Pa.	24,100	[2]40° 15' 17.0"	[2]76° 53' 11.0"
03049500	C9	Allegheny River at Natrona, Pa.	11,410	[2]40° 32' 10.0"	[2]79° 43' 07.0"
03049640	C10	Allegheny River at Lock and Dam 3 at Acmetonia, Pa.	11,592	[2]40° 32' 10.0"	[2]79° 48' 54.0"
		Nutrient Synoptic Stations[3]			
01540500	N1	Susquehanna River at Danville, Pa.	11,220	[2]40° 57' 29.0"	[2]76° 37' 10.0"
01550400	N2	West Branch Susquehanna River at Duboistown, Pa.	5,384	41° 13' 33.0"	77° 02' 37.0"
01553012	N3	West Branch Susquehanna River at Muncy, Pa.	6,457	41° 12' 18.0"	76° 48' 09.0"
01553018	N4	West Branch Susquehanna River at Montgomery, Pa.	6,471	41° 09' 57.0"	76° 52' 11.0"
01553025	N5	West Branch Susquehanna River at Allenwood, Pa.	6,496	41° 06' 29.0"	76° 53' 24.0"
01553115	N6	West Branch Susquehanna River at Watsontown, Pa.	6,580	[2]41° 04' 53.0"	[2]76° 51' 50.0"
01553500	N7	West Branch Susquehanna River at Lewisburg, Pa.	6,847	[2]40° 58' 03.0"	[2]76° 52' 36.0"
01554000	N8	Susquehanna River at Sunbury, Pa.	18,300	[2]40° 50' 04.0"	[2]76° 49' 37.0"
01554590	N9	Susquehanna River near Fishers Island at Selinsgrove, Pa.	18,434	40° 47' 57.0"	76° 50' 50.0"
015552108	N10	Susquehanna River at Hoover Island	19,007	40° 44' 35.0"	76° 50' 55.0"
01555270	N11	Susquehanna River at Dalmatia, Pa.	19,198	40° 39' 30.0"	76° 54' 35.0"
01555565	N12	Susquehanna River at Liverpool, Pa.	19,471	40° 34' 15.0"	76° 58' 02.0"
01555645	N13	Susquehanna River at Montgomery Ferry, Pa.	19,623	40° 30' 26.0"	76° 58' 16.0"
[1]01555710	C3	Susquehanna River below Clemson Island (Main Channel)	19,673	40° 27' 42.1"	76° 56' 56.1"
01564895	N14	Juniata River at Lewistown, Pa.	2,519	[2]40° 35' 40.0"	[2]77° 34' 58.0"
01565810	N15	Juniata River at Mifflintown, Pa.	2,840	[2]40° 34' 12.0"	[2]77° 24' 00.0"
01565812	N16	Juniata River at Port Royal, Pa.	2,848	40° 32' 06.0"	77° 22' 54.0"
01566290	N17	Juniata River at Thompsontown, Pa.	3,155	40° 33' 12.0"	77° 14' 15.0"

Table 4. Stations for collection of streamflow, continuous water-quality data, and nutrient synoptic samples, Pennsylvania, 2008.—Continued

[mi², square miles]

Station number	Map identifier	Station description	Drainage area (mi²)	Latitude	Longitude
01566350	N18	Juniata River at Millerstown, Pa.	3,177	40° 32' 05.0"	77° 09' 28.0"
[1]01567000	C5	Juniata River at Newport, Pa.	3,354	[2]40° 28' 42.0"	[2]77° 07' 46.0"
01567340	N19	Juniata River at Amity Hall, Pa.	3,405	40° 25' 39.0"	77° 00' 52.0"
01567330	N20	Susquehanna River near Duncannon, Pa.	19,728	40° 23' 59.0"	77° 00' 26.0"
01569100	N21	Susquehanna River at Marysville, Pa.	23,511	40° 20' 26.0"	76° 54' 58.0"
[1]01570500	C8	Susquehanna River at Harrisburg, Pa.	24,100	[2]40° 15' 17.0"	[2]76° 53' 11.0"
01571515	N22	Susquehanna River at Highspire, Pa.	24,337	40° 12' 16.0"	76° 48' 09.0"

[1]Station used for collection of continuous water-quality data and nutrient data.

[2]Horizontal coordinate information is referenced to the North American Datum of 1927.

[3]Two samples were collected at each station between June 11–12, 2008; one 100 feet from the left bank and the other 100 feet from the right bank. Latitudes and longitudes reported in this table represent the center of the river.

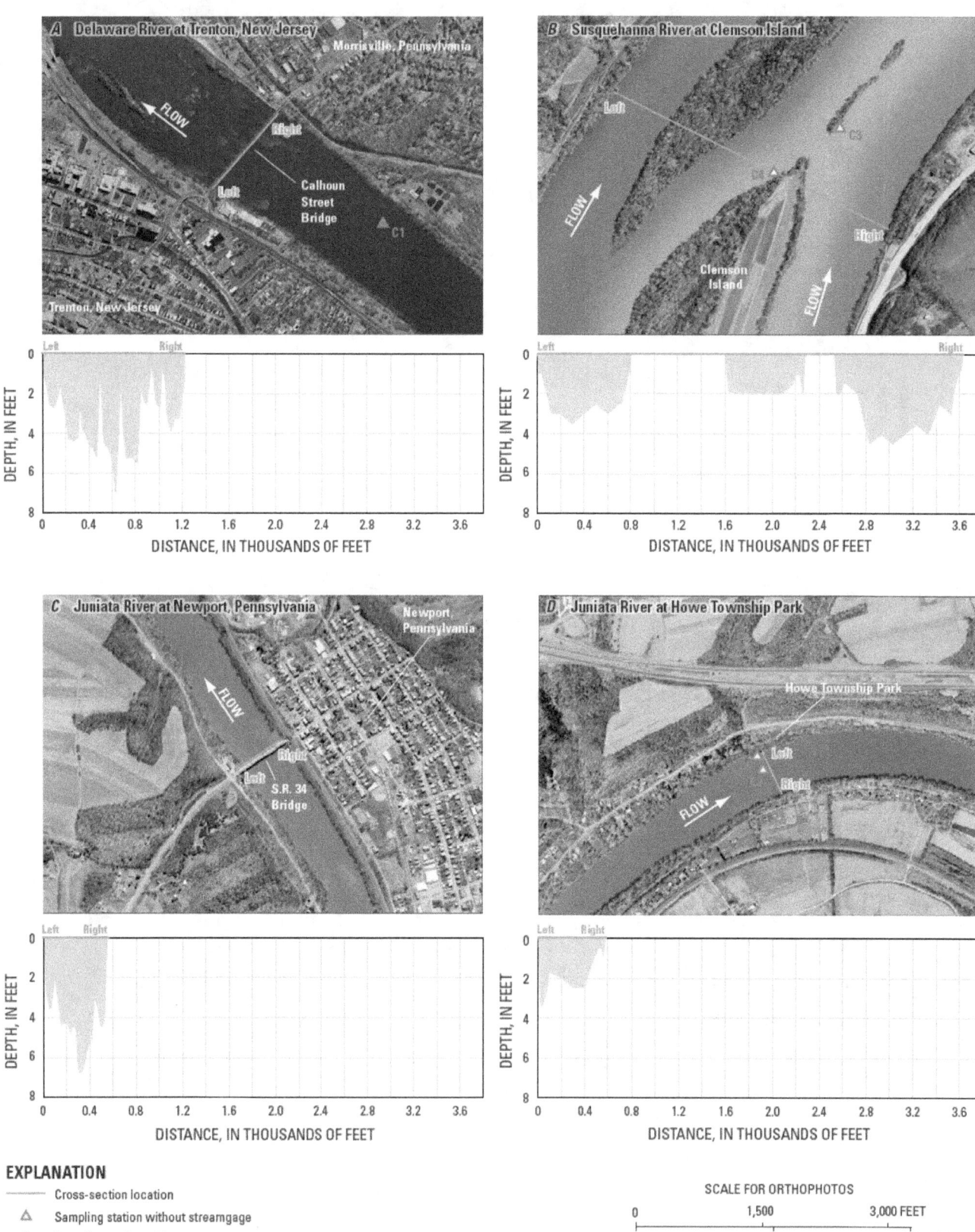

Figure 5.   Orthophotos and channel cross sections in the vicinity of selected continuous-monitoring stations in free-flowing reaches of the *A*) Delaware, *B*) Susquehanna, and *C* and *D*) Juniata Rivers, Pennsylvania.
[Orthophotos from Pennsylvania Spatial Data Access (2009), and New Jersey Office of Information Technology (2009)]

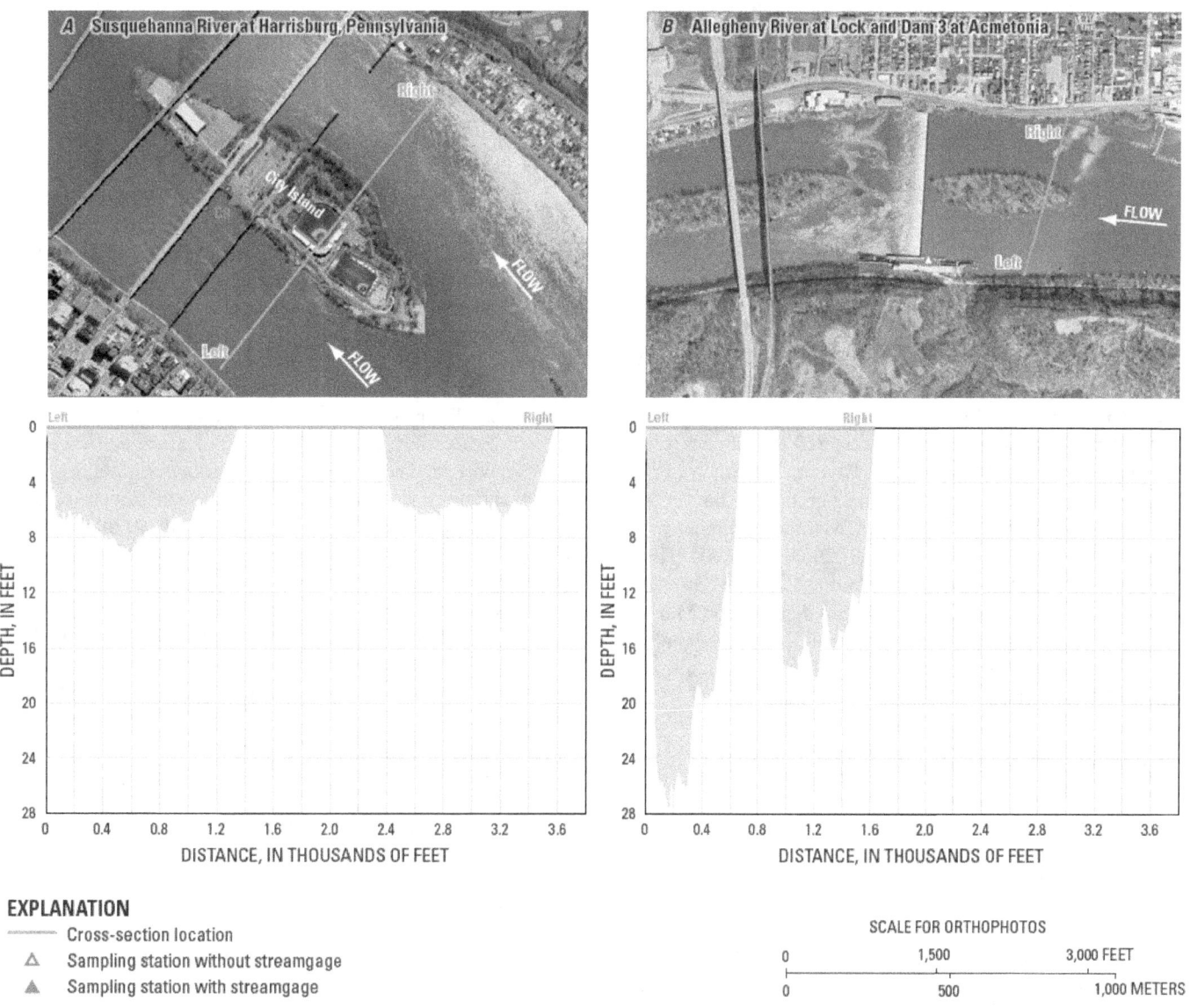

Figure 6.   Orthophotos and channel cross sections in the vicinity of selected continuous-monitoring stations in impounded reaches of the *A*) Susquehanna, and *B*) Allegheny Rivers, Pennsylvania.
[Orthophotos from Pennsylvania Spatial Data Access (2009)]

Juniata River in the Vicinity of Howe Township Park

The channel cross section at Howe Township is predominantly riffle habitat and is approximately 580 ft wide during base-flow conditions (fig. 5D). The maximum depth estimated for base-flow conditions on June 23, 2008, was 3.5 ft. The deepest part of the channel was within the YOY smallmouth-bass microhabitat near the left bank.

A sonde was deployed in the microhabitat on May 23, 2008, at station C6 (Juniata River near Howe Township Park [Microhabitat]) about 75 ft upstream of the cross section shown in fig. 5D and approximately 25 ft from the left bank. The microhabitat extends out for about 100 ft from the left bank and is protected by a gravel bar deposited just upstream. Water here is slow-moving compared to the riffle habitat in the rest of the cross section. Most of the area in the microhabitat is approximately 2 ft deep during base-flow conditions. Another sonde was deployed nearby in the main-channel habitat on June 4, 2008, at station C7 (Juniata River near Howe Township Park [Main Channel]). This sonde was approximately 190 ft from the left bank in a riffle characterized by relatively fast-moving water.

Susquehanna River at Harrisburg, Pennsylvania

The channel cross section of the Susquehanna River at Harrisburg, Pa., is within an impoundment 3,200 ft upstream of an 8-ft high, 3,000 ft wide dam that is notched out for about 33 ft on the left side. The cross section shown in fig. 6A represents the channel approximately 800 ft upstream from the sonde at station C8 (Susquehanna River at Harrisburg, Pa.). The width of the channel at this cross section is about 3,500 ft under normal base-flow conditions. Maximum depth estimated for base-flow conditions on June 23, 2008, was 9.2 ft. The channel on the left side of City Island is deeper and carries the majority of streamflow. The sonde was deployed on May 15, 2008, in a location characteristic of main-channel habitat, about 15 ft from the east shore of City Island in water that is about 3 ft deep during base-flow conditions.

Delaware River at Trenton, New Jersey

The channel of the Delaware River at Trenton (fig. 5A) was characterized from depth and width data collected during a base-flow measurement in June 2008 from the upstream side of the Calhoun Street bridge. Data collected during this measurement indicate the channel is approximately 1,200 ft wide and had an estimated maximum depth on June 23, 2008, of 7.0 ft. Velocities within this cross section varied from 0.56 to 2.41 ft/s; the average was 1.33 ft/s. Relatively shallow points shown in fig. 5A are the result of sandbar features upstream of bridge piers. The sandbar features are not present in the cross section at station C1 where the sonde was deployed. The

sonde was in a riffle about 1,780 ft upstream and about 365 ft from the right bank (Pennsylvania side of the river).

Allegheny River at Lock and Dam 3 at Acmetonia, Pennsylvania

The cross section at station C10 (Allegheny River at Acmetonia, Pa.) is heavily influenced by the C.W. Bill Young Lock and Dam (fig. 6B), which consists of a single lock chamber of the left side of the river and a concrete weir wall across the width of the river (U.S. Army Corps of Engineers, 2004). Under base-flow conditions, the dam backs water up to a maximum depth of approximately 28 ft (fig. 6B) in the vicinity of the sonde deployed at station C10. The sonde was deployed at a depth of approximately 5 ft during base-flow conditions.

Methods

Continuous Water-Quality Monitoring

All sondes deployed at each sampling station measured dissolved-oxygen concentration (in milligrams per liter), pH (in standard units), water temperature (in degrees Celsius), and specific conductance (in microsiemens per centimeter) every 30 minutes. Sondes at USGS stations at Harrisburg on the Susquehanna River and at Newport on the Juniata River were connected to existing instrumentation so near real-time data could be transmitted to the Internet and used to monitor water-quality conditions throughout the summer.

For this study, dissolved-oxygen measurements were most important. Therefore, newer and more reliable luminescent technology was used to determine the dissolved-oxygen concentration. All sondes except for one utilized this new technology. One sonde, deployed at the Shady Nook station, was equipped with a probe using older amperometric technology for dissolved oxygen. Each sonde was equipped with internal memory capable of storing the water-quality measurements. Set-up and calibration of the sondes followed manufacturer guidelines (Yellow Springs Instruments, 1999). In addition, a zero dissolved-oxygen solution (prepared on the day needed) was used to check the dissolved-oxygen performance of the sonde. Calibration values for independent field water-quality meters, which were used to check the measurements from the deployed sondes, were recorded in a logbook dedicated to that water-quality meter. Calibration values for the sondes deployed at each station were recorded on field data sheets for that station.

Sondes were serviced every 1 to 2 weeks following guidelines established by Wagner and others (2006). For servicing, freshly calibrated field water-quality meters were positioned with the deployed sonde to collect side-by-side measurements of water temperature, dissolved oxygen, pH, and specific conductance. The deployed sonde was then cleaned and returned to the water and a second set of side-by-side readings was recorded. These readings were used to adjust the measurements stored in the memory of the deployed sonde. Adjustments to the record were made following recommendations of Wagner and others (2006) using the USGS computer program Automated Data Processing System (ADAPS) (U.S. Geological Survey, 2003). Following the checks against the field water-quality meter, the deployed sondes were retrieved and the data downloaded to a field data logger.

Most of the sondes worked well throughout the project. However, the one sonde deployed in the Susquehanna River at Shady Nook Boat Launch (station C2), which utilized the older amperometric technology, had spotty performance, and some data were lost.

Statistical differences between microhabitat and main-channel stations were determined using the two-sided Wilcoxon signed-rank test (Helsel and Hirsch, 2002, p.142–147). The same test was also used to determine differences between data collected in 2008 and historical data from the 1970s. The Wilcoxon rank-sum test (Helsel and Hirsch, 2002, p. 118–124) was used for comparisons between the Susquehanna River and Delaware River and the Susquehanna River and Allegheny River. The null hypothesis for all tests was that there is no difference between median values of compared sites. For this report, the null hypothesis was rejected if the p-value was less than 0.05 (a less than 5 percent probability that a difference occurs by chance).

Nutrient Sampling

One of the largest oxygen-demanding in-stream processes is respiration from algae and rooted aquatic plants. Nutrients stimulate plant growth and, therefore, may be one of the factors that influence dissolved-oxygen concentrations. To evaluate spatial differences in nutrient concentrations, a one-time synoptic survey of 25 sampling locations (including 3 stations where sondes were deployed) in the Susquehanna River and tributaries was conducted on June 11 and 12, 2008 (fig. 7). Nutrient data collected as part of the Pennsylvania Black Fly Suppression Program indicate that for the mainstem of the Susquehanna River downstream from the confluence of the West Branch Susquehanna River, water chemistry is different for the west and east sides of the river (D. Rebuck, Pennsylvania Department of Environmental Protection, written commun., 2007). These data prompted a sampling strategy incorporating samples from both sides of the river.

Two separate depth-integrated samples, one 100 ft from the left bank and one 100 ft from the right bank at each of the 25 sampling locations (50 samples total), were collected using a DH-81 sampler following methods adapted from Wilde and others (1998). Samples were collected in pre-cleaned 3-L teflon bottles. Four subsamples were taken from the 3-L sample bottle. A 125-mL subsample collected for analysis of filtered ammonia nitrogen was filtered in the field using a flask-mounted suction device fitted with a 0.45 micron pore-size polyamid filter and fixed with sulfuric acid to a pH of less than 2. A second 125-mL subsample collected for analysis

of phosphorus and ammonia plus organic nitrogen was fixed with sulfuric acid without filtering. A third 125-mL sample collected for analysis of orthophosphate, nitrite nitrogen, and nitrate nitrogen was filtered without having any fixative added. A 500-mL subsample for total nitrogen was collected without filtration or fixation. All samples were chilled immediately. Laboratory analyses were performed by the PADEP laboratory.

In addition, samples for streambed sediment at right-bank and left-bank stations were collected for nutrient analyses. The samples were collected by inserting a teflon cylinder into the streambed sediment to a depth of 2 cm and then sliding a teflon wafer underneath the tube to hold the streambed sediment in place inside the tube. Five such streambed-sediment tubes were collected at each sampling station, combined in a stainless-steel bowl, and thoroughly mixed. A subsample of this mixture was then transferred into a 500 mL high-density polypropylene wide-mouth jar that was sealed and chilled. Laboratory analyses for ammonia plus organic nitrogen, ammonia, and phosphorus in the streambed sediment were conducted by the PADEP laboratory. Laboratory methods used for the analyses of streambed sediment are as follows: ammonia nitrogen in bottom material–EPA method 350.1; ammonia plus organic nitrogen in bottom material–EPA method 351.2; total phosphorus in bottom material–EPA method 365.1 (U.S. Environmental Protection Agency, 1993).

Biochemical Oxygen Demand Sampling

Along with the nutrient samples, a 500-mL subsample of the 3-L sample was poured into a pre-cleaned high-density polyethylene bottle at each station for analysis of BOD. BOD is a measure of the amount of organic pollution in water (Hem, 1985, p. 158). BOD is measured in milligrams per liter of oxygen and is typically used to determine the oxygen requirements of wastewaters (Alley, 2000, p. 3.19). As organic matter is decomposed or oxidized, the oxygen needed for the decomposition must come from the water. The purpose of these samples was to determine if there are oxygen-demanding materials present in the water that might cause oxygen deficits that are not related to community respiration. These BOD samples were not filtered and received no fixative, but they were chilled immediately. Samples were analyzed in the PADEP laboratory.

Quality Assurance

Protocols for calibrating, deploying, and servicing the continuous-monitoring sondes were derived from the manufacturer's instruction manual (Yellow Springs Instruments, 1999) and from Wilde and others (1998) and Wagner and others (2006). Log books for recording calibration, performance, and service information were prepared for each field instrument. Information in these log books was updated during each service visit for each instrument. Log-book records

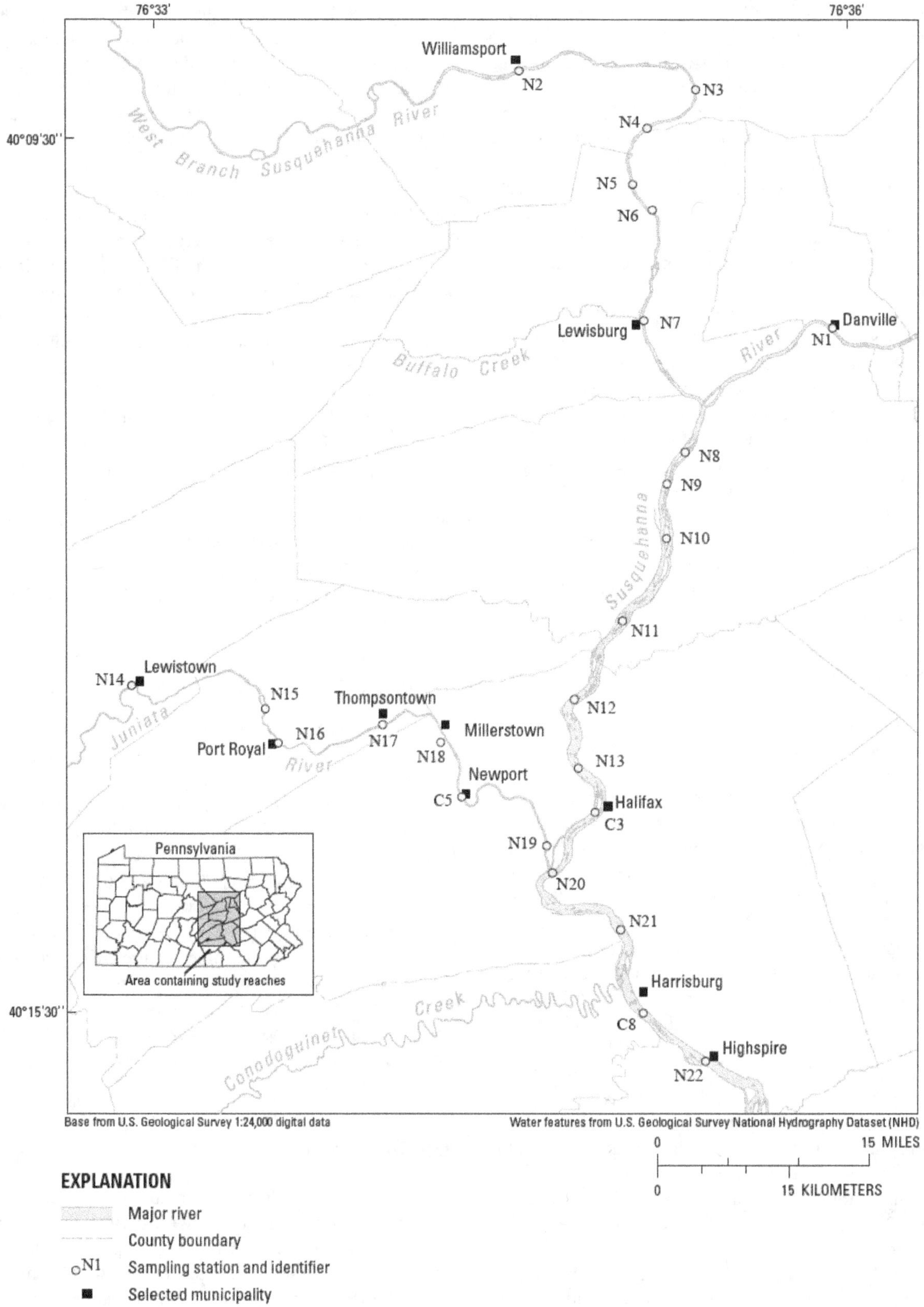

Figure 7. Locations of stations selected for the nutrient synoptic survey in the Susquehanna River Basin, Pennsylvania, June 11 and 12, 2008.

were used to document calibration accuracies and to track the performance of each instrument over the course of the project. Comprehensive field data sheets were used to record field observations and to ensure that all necessary field observations were completed.

Quality Control

Numerous quality-control measures were routinely adhered to during the project. Prior to the sampling season, thermistors for field instruments were checked for accuracy against a National Institute for Standards and Technology (NIST)-certified thermometer. Instruments for other field measurements (pH, specific conductance, and dissolved oxygen) were calibrated on the day of sampling. Only certified standards and buffers were used for calibrations. Buffers and standards were discarded if the expiration date had passed. One-point dissolved-oxygen calibrations were made using the air-saturation approach (Yellow Springs Instruments, 1999). Readings were adjusted for atmospheric pressure using a Thommen® pocket barometer that had been adjusted to National Weather Service readings and adjusted for the elevation at Harrisburg, Pa. A zero dissolved-oxygen solution of sodium sulfite and cobalt chloride, prepared fresh on the days it was needed, was used to check that the dissolved-oxygen meters were accurate at the low end of the range of expected dissolved-oxygen concentrations. Any meter that would not return a dissolved-oxygen reading of 0.3 mg/L or less in a zero dissolved-oxygen solution was not used.

Quality-control measures for the nutrient synoptic survey included submitting blank samples, duplicate samples, and reference samples for analysis of nutrients and BOD. A summary of all quality-control samples submitted for the project is presented in appendix 1.

Blank Samples

For the stream-water samples in the nutrient synoptic survey, six field blank samples (12 percent of all water nutrient samples collected) were submitted to the PADEP laboratory for nutrient analyses. The data-quality objective for the project was to determine if any constituents were measured at a concentration larger than the method detection limit in a blank sample. None of the constituents analyzed in the blank samples were measured at a concentration greater than the detection limit. The sample collected from the West Branch Susquehanna River at Duboistown, Pa., had a concentration of dissolved ammonia of 0.02 mg/L, which is the detection limit for this constituent. This concentration is comparable to most environmental samples collected during the study. All other results were lower than the detection limits. These results indicate that sampling procedures, sample containers, lab protocols, and cleaning procedures were not contributing contamination to the samples collected for the project. Blank samples were not submitted for bottom material.

Duplicate Samples

Field duplicate samples were used to identify the precision (reproducibility) of analytical results. Field duplicate samples were collected and processed immediately following each associated primary environmental sample (a sequential replicate), using identical procedures. For the duplicate samples, a relative percent difference (RPD) was calculated between the two samples according to the following equation:

$$RPD = (d/x) \times 100, \qquad (1)$$

where d is the difference in concentration between the primary environmental sample and the field duplicate sample, and x is the average concentration of the primary environmental sample and the field duplicate sample. The data-quality objective for the project was that all duplicate samples would have RPD values of 20 percent or less. An acceptance value of 20 percent for the RPD is commonly used for water-quality studies (for example, Allegheny County Sanitary Authority, 2008; Lombard and Kirchmer, 2004) and is the value supported by EPA in a Quality Assurance Plan that is a model for others to use (U.S. Environmental Protection Agency, 2009; Eagle Valley Environmental Program, 2005).

For the stream-water samples in the nutrient synoptic survey, four duplicate-sample pairs (8 percent of all water nutrient samples collected) were submitted for analysis. Except for ammonia, the RPD for every nutrient species analyzed in each duplicate-sample pair was less than 20 percent. The RPD for filtered ammonia from the West Branch Susquehanna River at Duboistown, Pa., was 40 percent. For this sample, the concentration of ammonia in the environmental sample was 0.02 mg/L and the concentration in the replicate sample was 0.03 mg/L. These low measured concentrations resulted in a large RPD, even though the actual difference was quite small. These results suggest that the precision in collecting and analyzing water samples for nutrients was within the data-quality objective, and data for the nutrient concentrations can be used with confidence.

For the streambed-sediment samples in the nutrient synoptic survey, five duplicate-sample pairs (10 percent of all streambed-sediment nutrient samples collected) were collected sequentially and submitted for analysis. Except for ammonia plus organic nitrogen in two samples, the RPD for every nutrient species analyzed in each duplicate-sample pair was less than 20 percent. The RPD for ammonia plus organic nitrogen from the Susquehanna River at Montgomery Ferry, Pa., and left bank was 93 percent. The RPD for ammonia plus organic nitrogen from the Susquehanna River near Duncannon, Pa., right bank was 33 percent. These results suggest that the precision in collecting and analyzing streambed-sediment samples for nutrients was usually within data-quality objectives and, with the exception of ammonia plus organic nitrogen, data for the nutrient concentrations can be used with confidence.

Reference Samples

Standard reference samples are used to monitor the overall performance of a laboratory. Reference samples are made up in large quantities in a laboratory and sent to many labs for analysis. Results from all the labs are compiled, and a most probable value is calculated for each analyte in the sample. For this study, one standard reference sample for nutrients was obtained from the USGS Branch of Quality Assurance and submitted to the PADEP laboratory for analysis. The performance of the PADEP lab was evaluated against the most probable value using the same RPD calculation used to evaluate duplicate samples. The data-quality objective for the project was that analyses for all constituents in reference samples would have RPD values of 20 percent or less. This objective was met for all nutrients measured where an RPD could be calculated. For ammonia plus organic nitrogen, an RPD could not be calculated. The most probable value for ammonia plus organic nitrogen in the standard reference sample was 0.675 mg/L. The PADEP lab returned a value of < 1.0 mg/L.

Monitoring Results and Implications, Susquehanna River

The acute effects of low dissolved-oxygen concentration (to 1.0 mg/L) on behavior and survival of a variety of fish are well characterized (Siefert and others, 1974; Spoor, 1984), but for this project, the interest is in assessing primarily dissolved-oxygen concentrations and water temperatures that may be stressful in YOY smallmouth-bass microhabitat. In addition to stress, lower velocity microhabitats may also be more conducive to proliferation and growth of opportunistic bacteria like *F. columnare,* further increasing the probability of infection. The link between environmental stressors and bacterial infection, although not directly tested as part of this study, is that stress compromises the immune system (Ripley and others, 2008) and thereby predisposes the young to infection. The national criteria for dissolved-oxygen concentrations were developed primarily using behavioral response (increased swimming activity or swimming to the surface, for example) to indicate stressful concentrations of dissolved oxygen. Studies used to arrive at these criteria indicate progressively more abnormal behavior as dissolved-oxygen concentrations are decreased and temperatures are increased. In some cases, the behavioral response is death, indicating lethally stressful conditions. In other cases, the behavioral response is temporary, and the fish resume normal activity when dissolved-oxygen concentrations are increased to more normal levels (Spoor, 1984; Siefert and others, 1974). Because most experimental tests have not exposed fish to daily sinusoidal cycles consistent with variability observed in this study, the effect of varying dissolved-oxygen concentration on fish is poorly understood (U.S. Environmental Protection Agency, 1986). Fish may be stressed by low dissolved oxygen for a period of hours at night and then recover with increasing dissolved oxygen. Little is known about recurring stress over a period of days or weeks in YOY smallmouth-bass microhabitats.

Comparison of Water Quality Observed in Young-of-the-Year Smallmouth-Bass Microhabitats and Main-Channel Habitats

In this section, water quality in microhabitats of the Susquehanna River at Clemson Island (station C4) and the Juniata River at Howe Township Park (station C6) is compared with water quality of corresponding nearby main-channel habitats (stations C3 in the Susquehanna River below Clemson Island and C7 in the Juniata River at Howe Township Park) preferred by larger, older fish. For most comparisons, dissolved-oxygen concentration, pH, and water temperature were significantly different (p-values less than 0.05) in the microhabitats compared to the main-channel habitats (table 5).

Dissolved Oxygen

Daily minimum dissolved-oxygen concentrations in YOY smallmouth-bass microhabitats in the Susquehanna River at station C4 and the Juniata River at C6 generally were lower than nearby main-channel habitats (figs. 8C and 9C). The average daily minimum dissolved-oxygen concentrations at C4 and C6 were 1.1 and 0.3 mg/L lower, respectively, than in the corresponding main-channel habitat during the critical period (table 6). The lowest dissolved-oxygen concentrations in the microhabitats during the critical period were 3.3 mg/L at station C4 (June 11, 2008) and 4.1 mg/L at station C6 (July 22, 2008) (table 6). The lowest instantaneous dissolved-oxygen concentrations in the main-channel habitats were 5.3 mg/L (Susquehanna River at station C3; July 31, 2008) and 4.6 mg/L (Juniata River at station C7; July 21 and 22, 2008).

The 7-day mean dissolved-oxygen concentrations at paired stations in the Susquehanna and Juniata Rivers remained above the 6.0 mg/L national criterion for protecting earlylife stages of warm-water fish (fig. 10A and B, appendix 2), but daily minimum dissolved-oxygen concentrations in both microhabitats and in the Juniata River main-channel habitat sometimes were lower than national dissolved-oxygen limits for protecting earlylife stages of warm-water fish (5.0 mg/L) (figs. 8C and 9C). Microhabitats had daily minimum dissolved-oxygen concentrations that were lower than the national criterion of 5.0 mg/L more often than the corresponding main-channel habitats. During the critical period, daily minimum dissolved-oxygen concentrations were less than 5.0 mg/L in microhabitat in the Susquehanna River at Clemson Island on 31 days (out of 92 days in the critical period) compared to no days in the corresponding main-channel habitat. The maximum time that dissolved oxygen was less than 5.0 mg/L lasted 8.5 hours. In the Juniata River, daily minimum dissolved-oxygen concentration in the microhabitat was less than 5.0 mg/L on 20 days compared to only 5 days

Table 5.   Statistical comparison of water quality in young-of-the-year smallmouth-bass microhabitats and main-channel habitats in the Susquehanna and Juniata Rivers, Pennsylvania, 2008.

[MH, Microhabitat; MC, Main Channel; °C, degrees Celsius; µS/cm, microsiemens per centimeter; mg/L, milligrams per liter; <, less than]

Constituent[1]	p-value[3]	
	Susquehanna River, Clemson MH compared to Susquehanna River, Clemson MC[2]	Juniata River, Howe Township MH compared to Juniata River, Howe Township MC[2]
Minimum water temperature (°C)	< 0.0001	< 0.0001
Maximum water temperature (°C)	.0395	< .0001
Water temperature range (°C)	< .0001	.3517
Mean water temperature (°C)	< .0001	< .0001
Minimum specific conductance (µS/cm)	.0246	< .0001
Maximum specific conductance (µS/cm)	.0823	< .0001
Specific conductance range (µS/cm)	.9773	.0008
Mean specific conductance (µS/cm)	.0044	< .0001
Minimum pH (standard units)	< .0001	.0010
Maximum pH (standard units)	< .0001	< .0001
pH range (standard units)	.8218	.0002
Median pH (standard units)	< .0001	< .0001
Minimum dissolved oxygen (mg/L)	< .0001	< .0001
Maximum dissolved oxygen (mg/L)	< .0001	< .0001
Dissolved oxygen range (mg/L)	.0354	< .0001
Mean dissolved oxygen (mg/L)	< .0001	< .0001
7-day mean minimum dissolved oxygen (mg/L)	< .0001	< .0001
7-day mean dissolved oxygen (mg/L)	< .0001	< .0001

[1]Summary statistics (minimum, maximum, mean, range, 7-day mean minimum, and 7-day mean) are based on daily values.

[2]Results of two-sided Wilcoxon signed-rank test.

[3]For this study, a statistically significant difference exists if the p-value is less than 0.05.

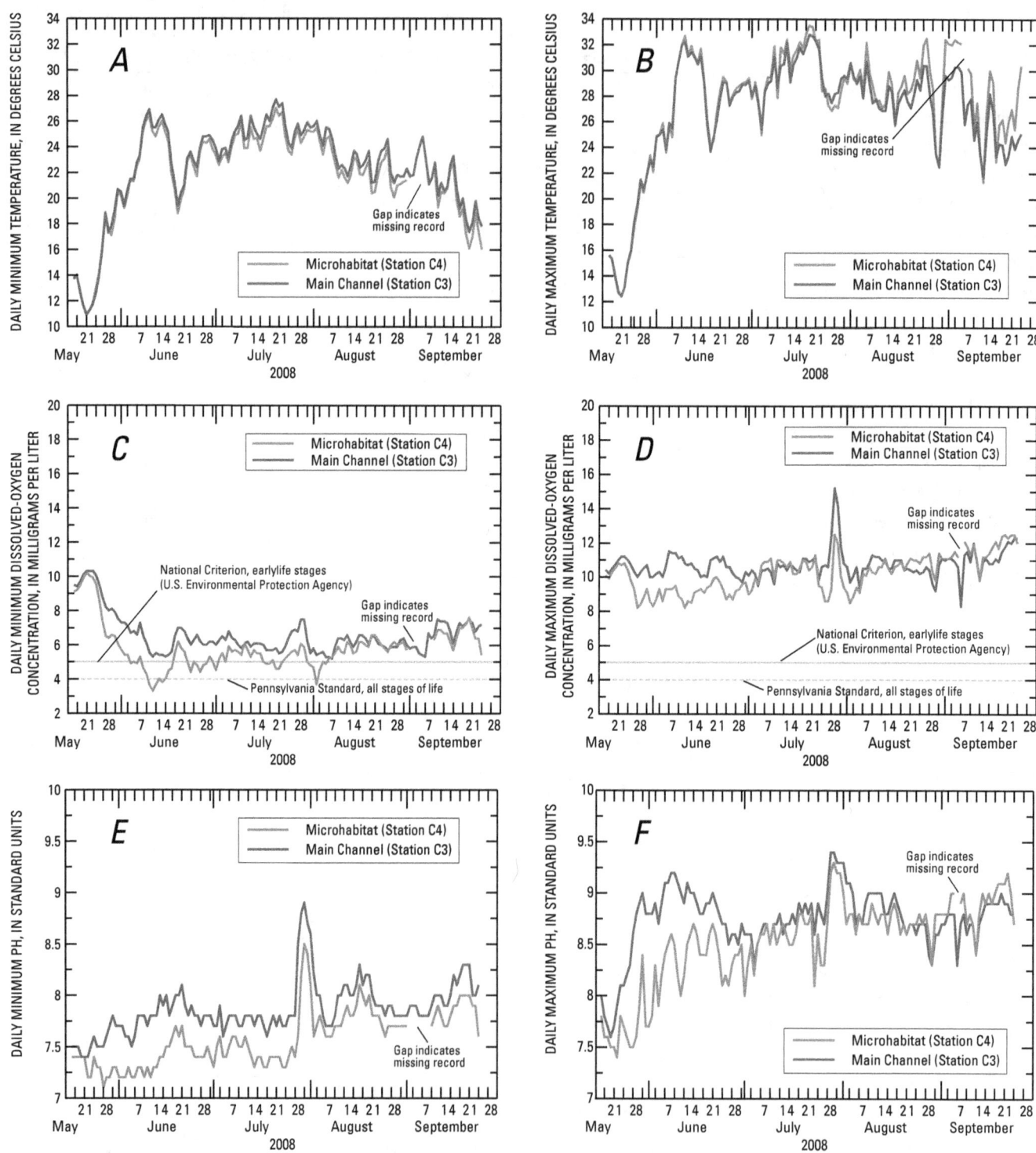

Figure 8.   Water quality in young-of-the-year smallmouth-bass microhabitat and main-channel habitats of the Susquehanna River in the vicinity of Clemson Island, Pennsylvania, 2008.

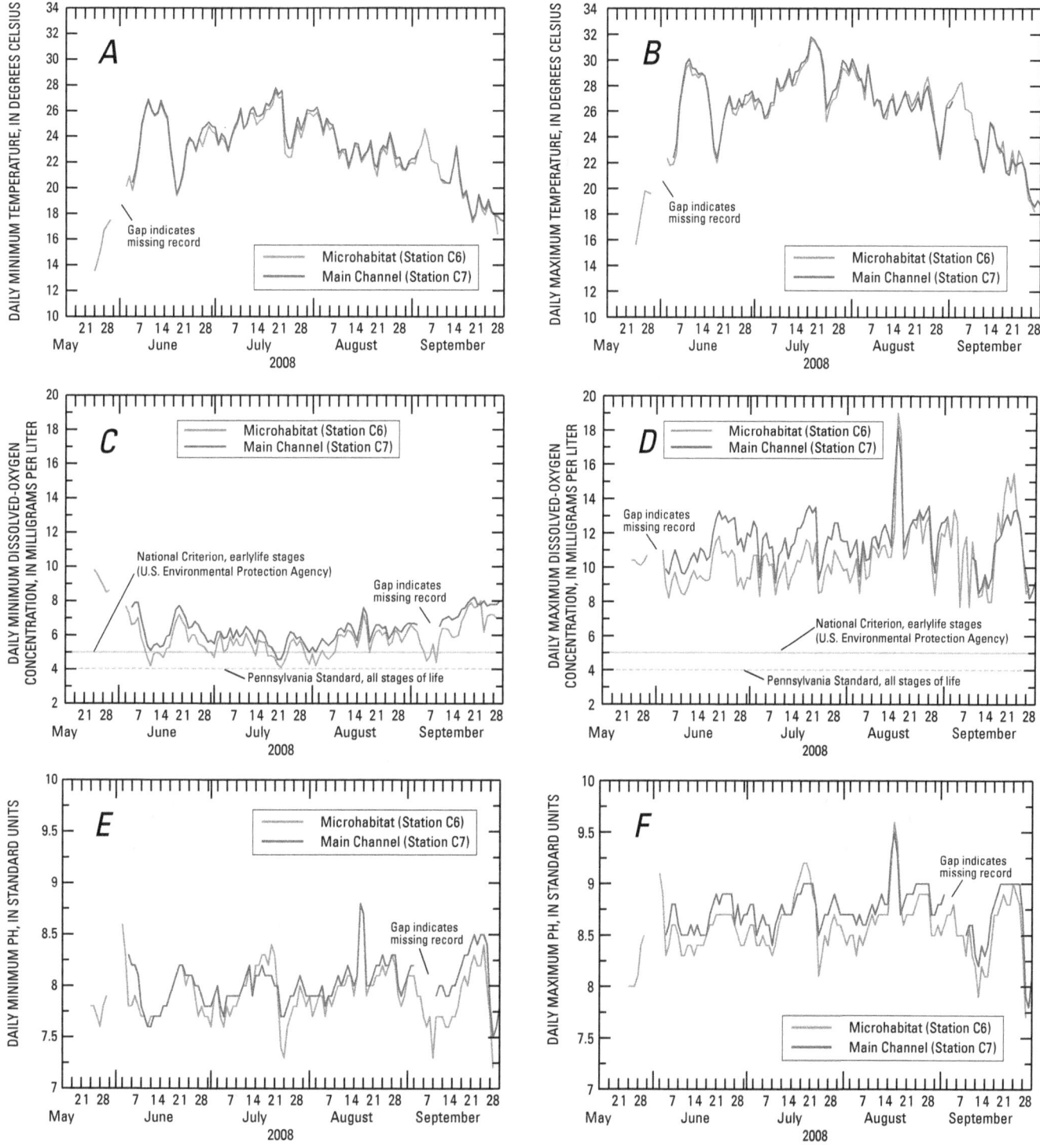

Figure 9.   Water quality in young-of-the-year smallmouth-bass microhabitat and main-channel habitats of the Juniata River in the vicinity of Howe Township Park, Pennsylvania, 2008.

Table 6. Summary statistics for water-quality data collected at selected stations in the Susquehanna River Basin, Pennsylvania, May 1 through July 31, 2008.

[C2, Susquehanna River at Shady Nook Boat Launch; C3, Susquehanna River below Clemson Island (Main Channel); C4, Susquehanna River at Clemson Island (Microhabitat); C5, Juniata River at Newport; C6, Juniata River near Howe Township Park (Microhabitat); C7, Juniata River near Howe Township Park (Main Channel); shading provided for comparison of young-of-the-year microhabitats and main-channel habitats; C, degrees Celsius; µS/cm, microsiemens per centimeter; mg/L, milligrams per liter; n, number of daily values; P25, 25th percentile; P75, 75th percentile; —, not computed]

Statistic	Daily minimum temperature (°C) Station						Daily mean temperature (°C) Station					
	C2	C3	C4	C5	C6	C7	C2	C3	C4	C5	C6	C7
n	15	76	76	81	65	57	15	76	76	80	65	57
Minimum	27.1	10.9	11.0	10.9	13.5	19.5	28.3	11.8	11.8	11.5	14.5	21.0
P25	28.2	20.7	20.4	18.3	22.6	23.6	29.5	22.5	22.4	18.8	24.1	25.0
Median	29.2	24.1	23.7	22.6	24.0	24.8	30.6	26.1	25.8	24.3	25.5	26.4
P75	30.4	25.5	24.9	24.0	25.8	26.0	31.6	27.6	27.4	26.0	27.3	27.6
Maximum	31.0	27.7	27.0	26.4	27.5	27.8	32.2	29.9	29.7	28.7	29.5	29.6
Mean	29.2	22.5	22.1	20.6	23.4	24.6	30.5	24.4	24.2	22.1	24.9	26.1
Standard deviation	1.3	4.5	4.2	4.7	3.1	1.9	1.3	4.8	4.7	5.1	3.3	2.0

Statistic	Daily maximum temperature (°C) Station						Daily temperature range (°C) Station					
	C2	C3	C4	C5	C6	C7	C2	C3	C4	C5	C6	C7
n	16	76	76	83	65	57	15	76	76	80	65	57
Minimum	29.5	12.4	12.4	12.0	15.6	22.4	2.0	1.0	1.1	.8	.9	1.6
P25	30.6	25.0	24.9	19.4	25.5	26.6	2.5	3.4	3.3	2.3	2.3	2.5
Median	32.1	28.4	28.5	25.9	26.9	27.8	2.7	4.3	4.8	3.1	3.0	3.2
P75	33.4	30.5	30.8	27.6	28.8	29.3	3.0	5.5	6.2	3.9	3.4	3.6
Maximum	33.9	32.8	33.5	31.2	31.5	31.8	3.5	6.8	7.9	5.9	6.3	5.2
Mean	32.0	26.7	26.8	23.4	26.4	27.7	2.7	4.2	4.7	3.1	3.0	3.1
Standard deviation	1.5	5.3	5.5	5.7	3.4	2.2	.4	1.4	1.9	1.2	.9	.8

Table 6.   Summary statistics for water-quality data collected at selected stations in the Susquehanna River Basin, Pennsylvania, May 1 through July 31, 2008.—Continued

[C2, Susquehanna River at Shady Nook Boat Launch; C3, Susquehanna River below Clemson Island (Main Channel); C4, Susquehanna River at Clemson Island (Microhabitat); C5, Juniata River at Newport; C6, Juniata River near Howe Township Park (Microhabitat); C7, Juniata River near Howe Township Park (Main Channel); shading provided for comparison of young-of-the-year microhabitats and main-channel habitats;   C, degrees Celsius; µS/cm, microsiemens per centimeter; mg/L, milligrams per liter; n, number of daily values; P25, 25th percentile; P75, 75th percentile; —, not computed]

Statistic	Daily minimum dissolved oxygen (mg/L)						Daily mean dissolved oxygen (mg/L)					
	Station						Station					
	C2	C3	C4	C5	C6	C7	C2	C3	C4	C5	C6	C7
n	—	76	76	74	65	57	—	76	76	74	65	57
Minimum	—	5.3	3.3	4.1	4.1	4.6	—	7.5	5.8	6.6	6.0	6.6
P25	—	6.0	4.9	5.7	5.0	5.5	—	8.0	7.0	8.1	7.2	8.2
Median	—	6.4	5.4	6.2	5.5	6.0	—	8.4	7.3	8.5	7.8	8.6
P75	—	7.3	5.9	7.7	6.1	6.4	—	8.9	7.8	9.4	8.3	9.0
Maximum	—	10.3	10.2	10.0	9.8	7.9	—	11.1	10.5	10.3	10.1	10.3
Mean	—	6.8	5.7	6.7	5.8	6.1	—	8.6	7.6	8.7	7.9	8.6
Standard deviation	—	1.4	1.6	1.5	1.3	.8	—	.9	1.1	.9	.9	.7

Statistic	Daily maximum dissolved oxygen (mg/L)						Daily dissolved oxygen range (mg/L)					
	Station						Station					
	C2	C3	C4	C5	C6	C7	C2	C3	C4	C5	C6	C7
n	—	76	76	74	65	58	—	76	76	74	65	57
Minimum	—	9.5	8.2	8.2	8.2	9.1	—	.6	.6	.3	.6	2.0
P25	—	10.3	9.1	10.3	9.3	10.5	—	3.3	3.3	3.1	3.4	4.5
Median	—	10.6	9.5	11.1	10.1	11.5	—	4.1	4.4	4.9	4.3	5.4
P75	—	11.0	10.5	12.2	10.7	12.5	—	4.9	5.0	5.9	4.8	6.3
Maximum	—	15.2	12.5	13.3	11.8	13.6	—	7.7	6.4	8.6	7.3	8.9
Mean	—	10.7	9.7	11.2	9.9	11.5	—	3.9	4.0	4.5	4.1	5.4
Standard deviation	—	.8	.9	1.1	.9	1.2	—	1.5	1.5	2.2	1.4	1.4

Table 6.   Summary statistics for water-quality data collected at selected stations in the Susquehanna River Basin, Pennsylvania, May 1 through July 31, 2008.—Continued

[C2, Susquehanna River at Shady Nook Boat Launch; C3, Susquehanna River below Clemson Island (Main Channel); C4, Susquehanna River at Clemson Island (Microhabitat); C5, Juniata River at Newport; C6, Juniata River near Howe Township Park (Microhabitat); C7, Juniata River near Howe Township Park (Main Channel); shading provided for comparison of young-of-the-year microhabitats and main-channel habitats; C, degrees Celsius; µS/cm, microsiemens per centimeter; mg/L, milligrams per liter; n, number of daily values; P25, 25th percentile; P75, 75th percentile; —, not computed]

Statistic	Daily minimum pH (standard units)						Daily median pH (standard units)					
	Station						Station					
	C2	C3	C4	C5	C6	C7	C2	C3	C4	C5	C6	C7
n	15	76	76	79	65	57	15	76	76	79	65	57
Minimum	7.2	7.4	7.1	7.3	7.3	7.6	7.4	7.5	7.3	7.5	7.6	7.9
P25	7.3	7.7	7.3	7.5	7.7	7.8	7.5	8.2	7.6	7.8	8.0	8.2
Median	7.3	7.8	7.4	7.6	7.8	7.9	7.6	8.3	7.8	8.0	8.2	8.4
P75	7.4	7.8	7.5	7.7	8.0	8.1	7.6	8.5	7.9	8.1	8.4	8.6
Maximum	7.5	8.9	8.5	8.3	8.6	8.3	7.8	9.2	9.0	8.5	9.0	8.7
Mean	7.3	7.8	7.4	7.6	7.9	7.9	7.6	8.3	7.8	8.0	8.2	8.4
Standard deviation	.1	.3	.2	.2	.2	.2	.1	.4	.3	.2	.3	.2

Statistic	Daily maximum pH (standard units)						Daily pH range (standard units)					
	Station						Station					
	C2	C3	C4	C5	C6	C7	C2	C3	C4	C5	C6	C7
n	15	76	76	79	65	57	15	76	76	79	65	57
Minimum	7.5	7.6	7.4	7.8	8.0	8.4	.1	.2	.1	.1	.2	.2
P25	7.9	8.6	8.1	8.2	8.4	8.6	.6	.8	.7	.6	.6	.7
Median	8.2	8.8	8.4	8.5	8.5	8.7	.8	.9	.9	.9	.7	.8
P75	8.3	8.9	8.6	8.7	8.7	8.8	.9	1.1	1.1	1.0	.8	.9
Maximum	8.3	9.4	9.3	9.2	9.2	9.0	1.0	1.5	1.6	1.3	1.4	1.1
Mean	8.1	8.7	8.3	8.4	8.6	8.7	.7	.9	.9	.8	.7	.8
Standard deviation	.3	.4	.4	.3	.3	.2	.3	.3	.4	.3	.2	.1

Table 6.   Summary statistics for water-quality data collected at selected stations in the Susquehanna River Basin, Pennsylvania, May 1 through July 31, 2008.—Continued

[C2, Susquehanna River at Shady Nook Boat Launch; C3, Susquehanna River below Clemson Island (Main Channel); C4, Susquehanna River at Clemson Island (Microhabitat); C5, Juniata River at Newport; C6, Juniata River near Howe Township Park (Microhabitat); C7, Juniata River near Howe Township Park (Main Channel); shading provided for comparison of young-of-the-year microhabitats and main-channel habitats; C, degrees Celsius; µS/cm, microsiemens per centimeter; mg/L, milligrams per liter; n, number of daily values; P25, 25th percentile; P75, 75th percentile; —, not computed]

Statistic	Daily minimum specific conductance (µS/cm)						Daily mean specific conductance (µS/cm)					
	Station						Station					
	C2	C3	C4	C5	C6	C7	C2	C3	C4	C5	C6	C7
n	15	76	76	81	65	57	15	76	76	80	65	57
Minimum	181	127	129	106	191	162	194	129	131	146	198	187
P25	233	224	225	179	265	241	256	229	237	197	281	263
Median	269	294	296	241	300	272	277	313	308	251	305	294
P75	288	317	319	256	307	298	301	326	327	265	313	306
Maximum	310	358	366	288	333	330	321	364	368	300	345	344
Mean	258	267	268	219	284	262	273	276	278	231	293	280
Standard deviation	41	67	66	46	35	46	38	69	67	44	33	37

Statistic	Daily maximum specific conductance (µS/cm)						Daily specific conductance range (µS/cm)					
	Station						Station					
	C2	C3	C4	C5	C6	C7	C2	C3	C4	C5	C6	C7
n	15	76	76	81	65	57	15	76	76	80	65	57
Minimum	215	130	133	157	202	214	10	2	3	2	3	3
P25	274	240	248	199	298	276	20	11	10	7	7	12
Median	289	319	318	256	311	304	29	16	17	13	12	16
P75	310	336	334	272	320	314	35	24	23	18	18	50
Maximum	344	368	369	305	355	354	74	61	69	169	125	96
Mean	289	286	287	238	300	293	31	19	20	19	17	31
Standard deviation	36	68	67	45	34	31	16	12	13	26	20	26

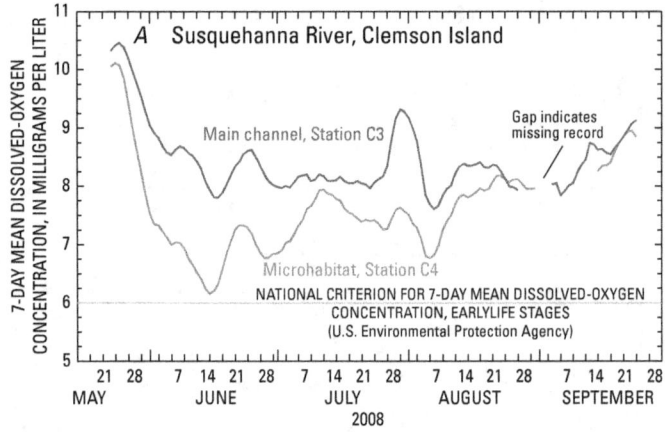

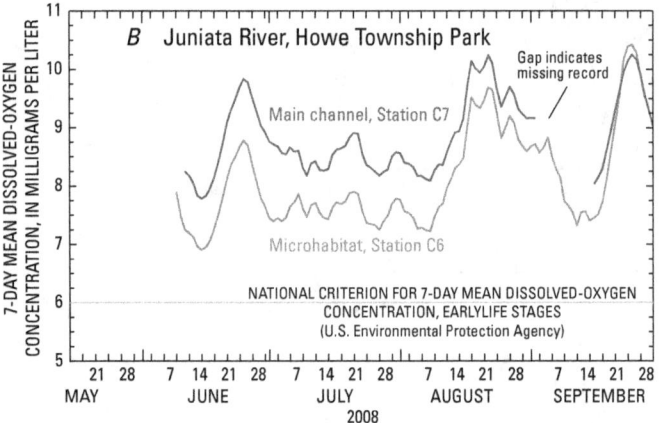

Figure 10. Seven-day mean dissolved-oxygen concentrations in *A*) the Susquehanna River in the vicinity of Clemson Island and *B*) the Juniata River in the vicinity of Howe Township Park, Pennsylvania, 2008.
[Value displayed on any day is the last day of the 7-day period.]

in the main-channel habitat. Dissolved-oxygen concentrations were below 5.0 mg/L longer in the microhabitat than in the main-channel habitat (the maximum time that dissolved oxygen was less than 5.0 mg/L in the microhabitat was 5.5 hours)

These data support the contention that YOY smallmouth bass in the study reaches are more likely to experience stress from sub-optimal dissolved-oxygen concentrations than older fish not living in or frequenting backwater and river-margin areas. Factors that may cause the lower dissolved-oxygen concentrations in microhabitats include lower reaeration rates relative to the main channel and respiration by aquatic biota. Respiration may consume oxygen more quickly in microhabitats than in the main channel because depths generally are lower, resulting in less volume of water compared to the main channel. Also, mixing with water from the main channel that potentially has more dissolved oxygen is slow because velocities are lower than those in the main channel.

Water Temperature

Rates of activity and physiological processes in smallmouth bass and other fish are influenced primarily by water temperature (Schreer and Cooke, 2002). The upper and lower thermal tolerances of different fish vary greatly and are flexible because fish may acclimate seasonally to different extremes (Barans and Tubb, 1973; Beitinger and others, 2000). The ability of smallmouth bass to acclimate to increasing temperature makes it difficult to determine a specific water-temperature threshold where stress may occur. While assigning a specific value that elicits a physiological or behavioral stress response is untenable, it is well established that increasing water temperature may contribute directly or indirectly to stress in YOY smallmouth bass by 1) lower solubility of dissolved oxygen (fig. 4), 2) direct stress resulting from an inability to acclimate to warming water temperatures, 3) greater populations of *F. columnare* and other pathogens, 4) magnified physiological and behavioral response to other stressors (Spoor, 1984), and 5) higher probability of impaired gill function because of enhanced adhesion of *F. columnare* to gill tissue (Decostere and others, 1999).

The implications of water temperature in microhabitats compared to the main channel are varied. Microhabitats did not always have warmer water temperatures than the main channel and are, therefore, not necessarily lower in dissolved oxygen or otherwise more stressful solely because of water temperature. Site-specific variables like exposure to sunlight and upstream inputs may have factored greatly in determining differences between water temperature of microhabitats and main-channel habitats.

The microhabitat in the Susquehanna River at station C4 was on the east side of Clemson Island (fig. 5), providing for exposure to sunlight for most of the day. This resulted in minimum, median, and maximum daily water temperatures that were comparable to the main-channel station at C3, which received similar exposure to sun. For example, mean daily water temperatures had medians of 25.8°C at station C4 and 26.1°C at station C3, and maximum daily water temperatures had medians of 28.5°C at C4 compared to 28.4°C at C3 (table 6). Median daily water-temperature range was 0.6°C greater (p-value < 0.0001; table 5) in the microhabitat compared to the main channel (fig. 11).

The microhabitat in the Juniata River at station C6 was shaded for most of each day by a canopy of trees, and mixing with faster-moving water in the main channel was poor under low to moderate streamflow conditions. These two factors allowed the microhabitat to maintain cooler temperatures compared to the main channel (p-value < 0.0001; table 5). Daily maximum water temperature in the microhabitat at station C6 had a median of 26.9°C compared to 27.8°C in the main channel at station C7 (table 6). Maximum instantaneous water temperature in the main-channel habitat was 31.8°C (July 19, 2008) compared to 31.5°C in the microhabitat. Daily water-temperature range (fig. 12) was statistically equivalent in both settings (p-value = 0.3517; table 5).

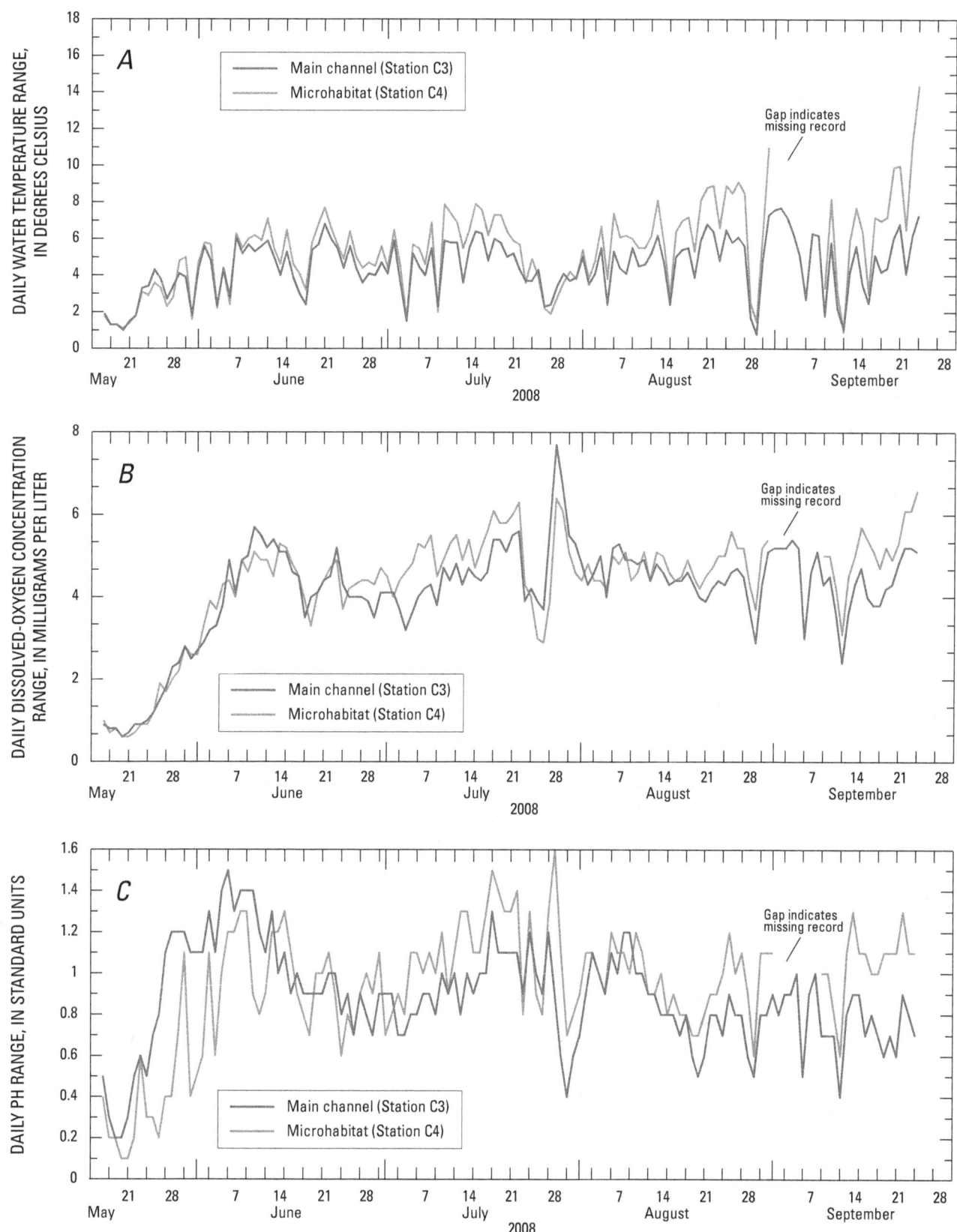

Figure 11. Daily range in water temperature, dissolved-oxygen concentration, and pH in the Susquehanna River in the vicinity of Clemson Island, Pennsylvania, 2008.

pH

During the critical period of May 1 through July 31, pH was near-neutral or alkaline at all stations in microhabitats and main-channel habitats (table 6). Daily pH minima, maxima, and medians in the microhabitats were up to 0.5 pH units lower (figs. 8E, 8F, 9E, and 9F) than the corresponding main-channel habitats (p-values < 0.0001 to 0.0010; table 5) but daily ranges were comparable (median daily range was 0.7 to 0.9 pH units in microhabitat and main-channel habitats; table 6). The median daily median pH in the Susquehanna River microhabitat at station C4 was 7.8 compared to 8.3 in the main channel at station C3. The median daily median pH value in the Juniata microhabitat at station C6 was 8.2 compared to 8.4 in the main channel. Somewhat longer exposure to sunlight and the resulting increased productivity may explain why pH values are greater in the main-channel habitats relative to the microhabitats.

Despite significant statistical differences between pH of microhabitats and main-channel habitats (table 5), the biological significance is unclear. Most studies of pH effects on smallmouth bass have focused on survival (Hill and others, 1988) and foraging behavior (Hill, 1989) in acidic (pH less than 6.0) environments. Smallmouth bass young (3 to 36 days post swim up) are sensitive to acidic pH and experience appreciable declines in survival rates at pH 5.7 compared to pH 7.4 (Hill and others, 1988). Potential stress during the critical period that may result from acute exposure to alkaline pH values (up to pH 9.4; fig. 8F) and large daily fluctuations (up to 1.6 pH units; table 6) as observed in the microhabitats and the main-channel habitats of the Susquehanna and Juniata Rivers is not well characterized.

A search of the scientific literature produced no studies focusing on the effects of alkaline environments on YOY smallmouth bass; however, Scott and others (2005) investigated the effect of high pH (up to pH 10.54) on ion balance, ammonia excretion, and behavior of perch (*Perca fluviatilis*), a warm-water fish that commonly coexists with smallmouth bass in lake habitats. Perch inhabiting alkaline lake waters (pH of 9.9) had three times more plasma ammonia compared to fish from neutral waters, indicating the fish were stressed because of a disruption of the ability to excrete ammonia (waste) (Scott and others, 2005). Despite apparently stressful pH levels, radio-tracking results indicated that adult perch and pike (*Esox lucius*) did not seek refuge in nearby water of neutral pH. Scott and others (2005) concluded that the benefits of withstanding the alkaline pH conditions were greater (better foraging, less predation) than the benefit of moving into more pH-neutral water.

The relevancy and implications of these findings on YOY smallmouth bass in the study reaches are unclear. Smallmouth bass typically inhabit waters with pH levels of 5.7 to 9.0, although the optimal pH range is 7.9 to 8.1 (Edwards and others, 1983). In this study, YOY smallmouth bass were exposed to pH that changed by as much as 1.6 units in a day (table 6) but rarely were exposed to alkaline pH that exceeded

9.0 during the critical period (figs. 8E, 8F, 9E, and 9F). Values of 9.0 or greater were only sustained for periods of less than 12 hours. It seems unlikely that pH is a major stressor to YOY smallmouth bass in the study reaches, but perhaps when combined with temperatures that are relatively high and dissolved-oxygen concentrations that are below national criteria, alkaline pH and (or) large daily fluctuations in pH may contribute to overall stress.

Specific Conductance

Specific conductance is a measure of the capacity of dissolved ions in water to conduct an electrical current (Wilde and others, 1998). It is related to the dissolved solids concentration (Hem, 1985, p. 67) and can be used as a qualitative measure to distinguish between waters with high and low concentrations of dissolved solids. Ions dissolved in the water that may contribute to specific conductance include dissolved nutrients and metals. Nutrient and metal concentrations are known to fluctuate in concentration during the day (Scholefield and others, 2005; Nimick and others, 2005) in response to changes like those observed in this study for water temperature, pH, and dissolved oxygen. This daily cycling may be responsible for some of the inconsistent data observed in specific conductance.

During the critical period, average daily mean specific conductance was similar in microhabitats and main-channel habitats near Clemson Island (287 µS/cm compared to 286 µS/cm) but was greater in microhabitat at Howe Township Park compared to the main channel (300 µS/cm compared to 293 µS/cm). Minimum daily mean specific conductance in the microhabitat and main-channel habitat at Clemson Island were 131 µS/cm (May 20 and 21, 2008) and 129 µS/cm (May 20 and 21, 2008) compared to maximum values of 368 µS/cm (July 16, 2008) and 364 µS/cm (July 16, 2008), respectively. Specific conductance values at Howe Township Park were not as low (mean daily minima in the microhabitat and main-channel habitat were 198 µS/cm (May 24, 2008) and 187 µS/cm (June 24, 2008), respectively) or as high (maxima were 345 µS/cm (July 10, 2008) in microhabitat and 344 µS/cm (July 10, 2008) in main-channel habitat) as those for the Susquehanna River at Clemson Island.

Influence of Warm-Water Discharge at Shady Nook

Stream water at station C2 had an average daily maximum temperature of 32°C but daily maximums were only determined for 16 days (table 6) near the end of the critical period (July 16–31). During this time period, daily mean water temperature was 2–3°C warmer at station C2 than at station C3 below Clemson Island (fig. 13) indicating any stress resulting from other factors is likely to be magnified by the warm-water discharge. The sonde deployed as station C2 was about 15 ft from the right bank and was directly within the influence

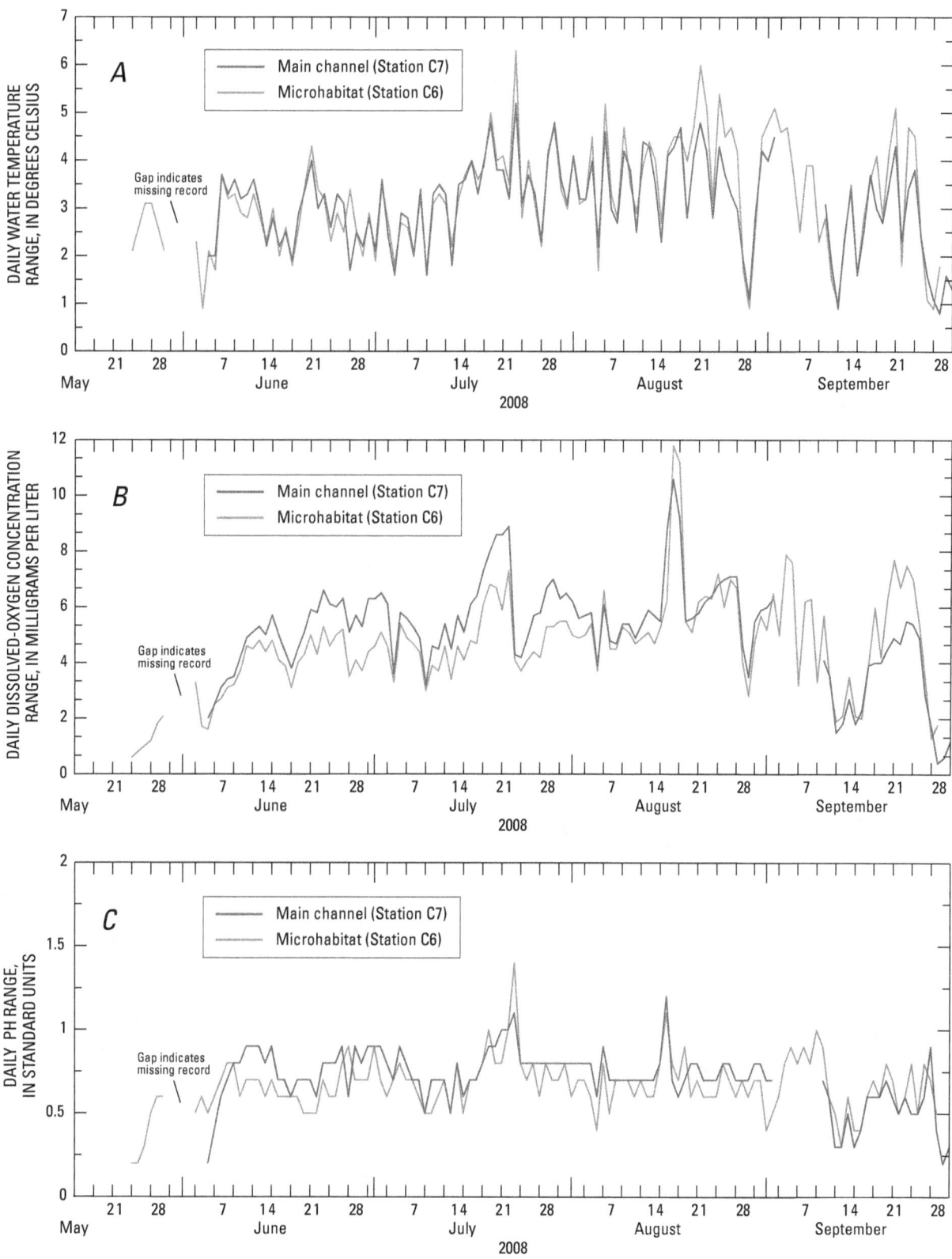

Figure 12. Daily range in water temperature, dissolved-oxygen concentration, and pH in the Juniata River in the vicinity of Howe Township Park, Pennsylvania, 2008.

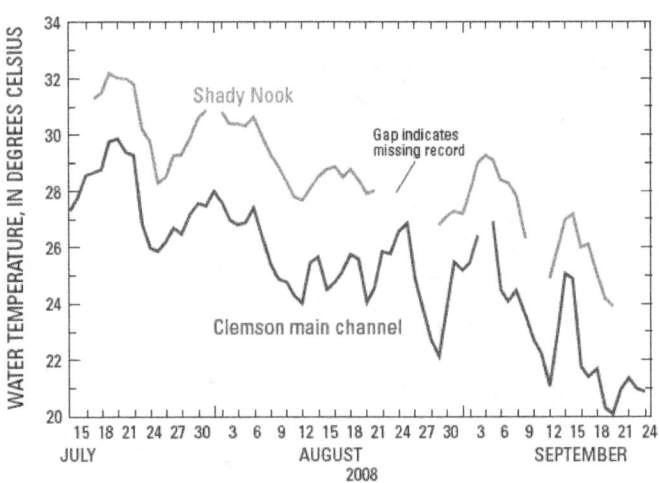

Figure 13. Comparison of mean daily water temperatures downstream of a warm-water discharge with mean daily water temperature at Clemson Island, Pennsylvania, July–September 2008.

of the warm-water discharge. It was not determined how far from the right bank the warm-water discharge affects the river temperature.

The warm-water discharge influencing water temperature at station C2 is about 30 mi upstream of Clemson Island. Because of heat dissipation between stations C2 and C3, groundwater inputs, and mixing with cooler water in the main channel of the Susquehanna River and tributaries entering on the right bank, it is unlikely that the warm-water discharge at station C2 has an effect on water temperature as far downstream as Clemson Island.

Spatial Variability of Nutrients in Selected Reaches in the Susquehanna River Basin

Nutrients are relatively not toxic to aquatic life, except at concentrations much larger than are commonly observed in the Susquehanna River and its tributaries. However, nutrients in streams contribute to plant growth, both rooted aquatic plants and periphyton. Excessive nutrient concentrations can lead to excessive plant growth. Over a 24-hour period, plants go through a daily cycle of photosynthesis and respiration that causes fluctuations in dissolved oxygen. If plant growth is excessive, the daily fluctuations in dissolved oxygen can become stressful or even lethal to fish. Therefore, an understanding of nutrient concentrations in the Susquehanna River study reaches may contribute to understanding stressful conditions that lead to the observed bacterial infections.

A one-time survey was conducted on June 11 and 12, 2008, for nutrients in water and streambed sediments. During the 2-day period, samples were collected from the right bank and left bank at 25 stations on the West Branch Susquehanna River, Juniata River, and mainstem Susquehanna River (fig. 7). In water samples, concentrations were determined

for ammonia plus organic nitrogen, ammonia nitrogen, nitrite nitrogen, nitrate nitrogen, total nitrogen, orthophosphate phosphorus, and total phosphorus. Orthophosphate phosphorus and filtered nitrate nitrogen are considered to be the nutrient species most readily available for plant growth (Vollenweider, 1968). Therefore, the discussion of nutrient concentrations in water will focus on orthophosphate phosphorus and nitrate nitrogen. For streambed-sediment samples, concentrations of ammonia plus organic nitrogen, total ammonia nitrogen, and total phosphorus were measured. The nutrient data from the entire survey for both water and streambed sediments are presented in appendix 3 in tables 3-1, 3-2, and 3-3.

Nitrogen in Water

Nutrient concentrations in the study reaches varied widely among the sampling locations. Considering all sampling stations, the highest concentration of nitrate nitrogen measured in water during the survey was in the sample collected from the right bank of the mainstem Susquehanna River at Harrisburg (fig. 14; appendix 3, table 3-3). This sampling station is about 1.7 mi downstream from the mouth of the Conodoguinet Creek. The Conodoguinet Creek receives inputs from five wastewater-treatment plants each having a designed flow of 1.0 Mgal/d or larger (Pennsylvania Department of Environmental Protection, 2009b). It is likely that the concentration of nitrate nitrogen in this sample was strongly influenced by water from the Conodoguinet Creek. The second highest concentration of nitrate nitrogen (2.08 mg/L) was in the sample collected from the left bank of the mainstem Susquehanna River at Highspire (station N22) (fig. 14; appendix 3, table 3-3). Samples from this location are believed to be influenced by effluent from the Harrisburg wastewater-treatment facility.

For the West Branch Susquehanna River, concentrations of nitrate nitrogen were similar for right-bank and left-bank samples, except for the sample from Lewisburg, which was twice as high as the next highest sample. Other concentrations of nitrate nitrogen in the West Branch fell within a narrow range from 0.41 to 0.74 mg/L (fig. 14; appendix 3, table 3-1).

For the Juniata River, concentrations of nitrate nitrogen were approximately twice as high as in the West Branch. Concentrations of nitrate nitrogen varied little from station to station. The highest concentration in the Juniata River samples was 1.42 mg/L, and the lowest concentration was 1.06 mg/L. Differences between left-bank and right-bank samples were minor (fig. 14; appendix 3, table 3-2).

For the mainstem of the Susquehanna River, concentrations of nitrate nitrogen were less than 1.0 mg/L for all stations except the two previously mentioned at Harrisburg (station C8, right bank) and at Highspire (station N22, left bank) where higher concentrations were suspected of being influenced by wastewater inputs. Concentrations in the mainstem were similar to concentrations in the West Branch but were only about half as large as concentrations in the Juniata River. Higher concentrations in the mainstem were expected in the left-bank

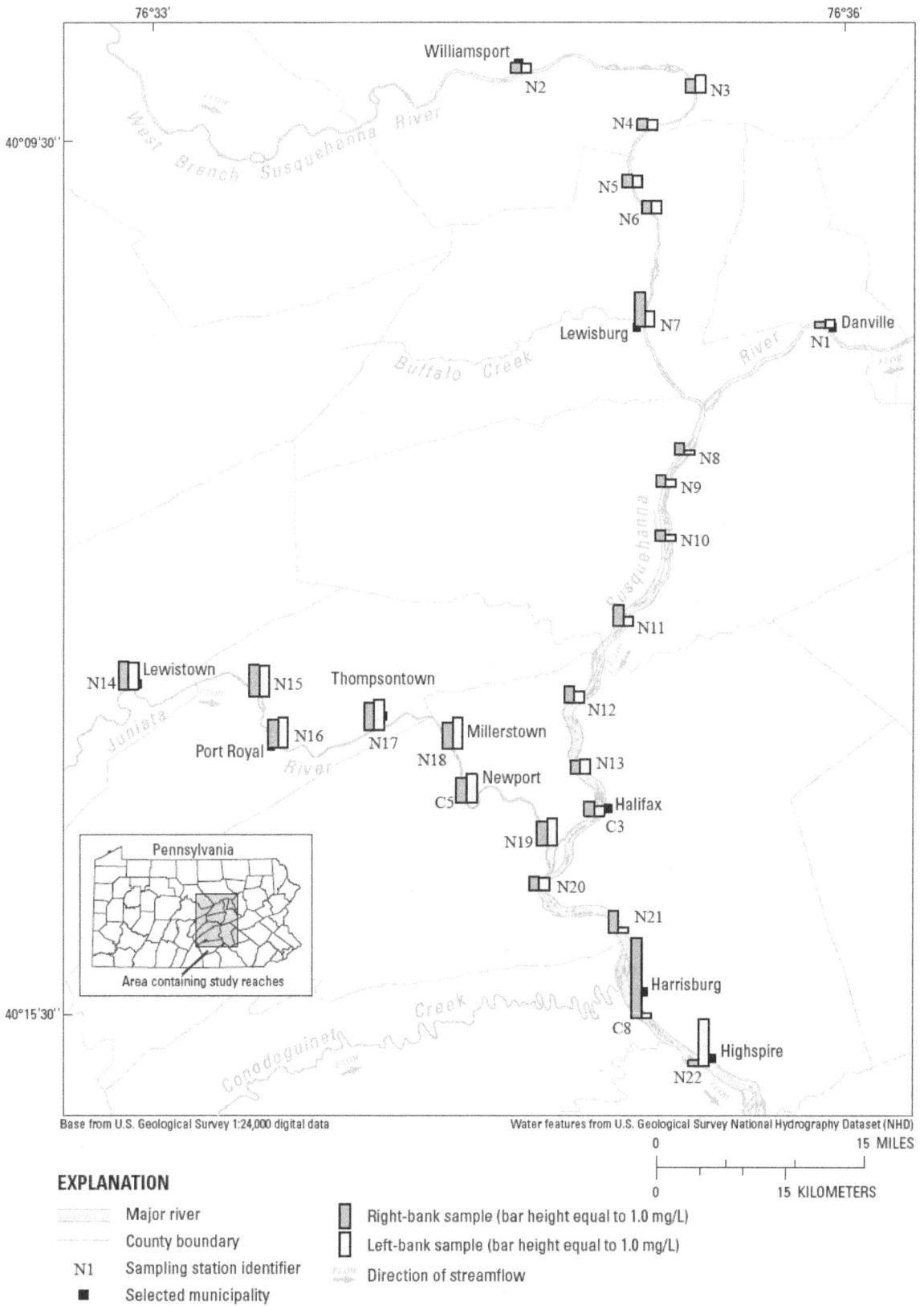

Figure 14. Relative comparison of nitrate nitrogen concentrations in water from selected reaches of the Susquehanna River and major tributaries, Pennsylvania, June 11 and 12, 2008.

samples, based on data from the Pennsylvania Black Fly Suppression Program (D. Rebuck, Pennsylvania Department of Environmental Protection, oral commun., December 10, 2007); however, the data from this study indicate the opposite. Concentrations of nitrate nitrogen were higher for right-bank samples than left-bank samples at 9 of the 12 sampling stations (fig. 14).

Concentrations of ammonia nitrogen in water were very low at all stations and varied from less than detection limits to 0.06 mg/L. Low ammonia concentrations in stream water are typical because ammonia is quickly oxidized to nitrite and then to nitrate when oxygen is present. Concentrations of ammonia plus organic nitrogen in water were below detection limits at every sampling station.

Concentrations of total nitrogen ranged from 0.7 mg/L (West Branch Susquehanna River at Duboistown (station N2) and Susquehanna River near Fishers Island (station N9)) to 3.77 mg/L (mainstem Susquehanna River at Harrisburg (station C8, right bank)). The downstream-most station at Highspire (station N22) on the left bank had a concentration of total nitrogen of 2.08 mg/L. Other than at Harrisburg, the highest concentrations of total nitrogen were in the Juniata River and ranged from 1.46 to 1.86 mg/L (appendix 3, tables 3-1, 3-2, 3-3).

Phosphorus in Water

The highest concentration of filtered orthophosphate phosphorus measured during the 2-day survey was 0.035 mg/L in the sample from the right bank of the West Branch Susquehanna River at Lewisburg (fig. 15; appendix 3, table 3-1). This sample was collected about 1,000 ft downstream from the mouth of Buffalo Creek. It is likely that the 100-ft distance from shore for this sample did not avoid collecting primarily Buffalo Creek water. Buffalo Creek receives effluent from several wastewater-treatment facilities, including a 3.75 Mgal/d designed-flow plant (Kelly Township Municipal Authority) that empties into Buffalo Creek near the mouth (T. Randis, Pennsylvania Department of Environmental Protection, oral commun., July 13, 2009). Therefore, water from Buffalo Creek may be expected to have higher nutrient concentrations than water from the West Branch Susquehanna River. The second highest concentration of filtered orthophosphate phosphorus measured during the 2-day survey was 0.028 mg/L in the sample from the left bank of the mainstem Susquehanna River at Highspire. This station is approximately 3.8 mi downstream from the wastewater-treatment plant effluent from the City of Harrisburg. This treatment facility has a designed flow of 37.7 Mgal/d (Pennsylvania Department of Environmental Protection, 2009b) and is the largest wastewater-treatment facility that discharges directly to the Susquehanna River. Effluent from this facility likely influenced phosphorus concentrations in samples collected at the Highspire sampling station.

For the West Branch Susquehanna River, concentrations of orthophosphate phosphorus were less than 0.01 mg/L for all sampling stations except for the right-bank sample from Lewisburg (station N7). Concentrations of total phosphorus were less than 0.020 mg/L except for the right-bank sample at Lewisburg (0.060 mg/L) and the right-bank sample at Duboistown (station N2) (0.034 mg/L). Concentrations were similar for right bank and left bank samples, except for the samples from Lewisburg and Duboistown.

In general, concentrations of phosphorus are higher in the Juniata River than in the West Branch Susquehanna River or in the mainstem Susquehanna River. Concentrations of orthophosphate phosphorus were larger than the detection level of 0.01 mg/L at all sampling stations. Concentrations ranged from 0.013 to 0.027 mg/L. Differences between left-bank and right-bank samples were small. Concentrations of total phosphorus ranged from 0.03 to 0.048 mg/L for the Juniata River sampling stations. As with orthophosphate, differences between left-bank and right-bank samples were small.

Biochemical Oxygen Demand in Water

Concentrations of BOD in untreated wastewaters typically range between 150 and 450 mg/L (Salvato, 1992, p. 479). Treated wastewaters commonly have BOD concentrations of 20 mg/L or less. Moderately polluted rivers might have BOD concentrations of 2–8 mg/L (Sawyer and others, 2003). Concentrations of BOD were low throughout the study reaches. The highest concentration was measured in the sample from the Susquehanna River at Danville (left bank), where the concentration was 3.7 mg/L. The next highest concentration was 3.4 mg/L in the sample from the Susquehanna River at Hoover Island, Pa. (left bank). Of the 50 samples collected during the survey, 38 had BOD concentrations less than 2.0 mg/L. These data indicate that dissolved-oxygen concentrations below the national criterion of 5.0 mg/L were not likely to have been caused by oxygen-demanding materials in the water.

Nutrients in Streambed Sediments

Nutrient concentrations in streambed sediments were even more variable than nutrients in water. This may be a reflection of the nature of the sediments available for sampling rather than the nutrient regime of the sampling location. Nutrients (particularly phosphorus) tend to sorb to fine-grained particles. Therefore, a sampling location having finer-grained sediment deposits may have higher nutrient concentrations than a location having more coarse sediment deposits. The sampling protocol for the nutrient synoptic survey called for collecting fine-grained sediment samples, but the grain size of the samples actually collected varied substantially from station to station.

For the survey, the highest concentration of total phosphorus in streambed sediments was 1.43 g/kg measured in the sample from the left bank of the Susquehanna River at Liverpool (station N12). The second highest concentration of total phosphorus was 1.04 g/kg in the sample from the right bank of the Susquehanna River at Harrisburg (station C8).

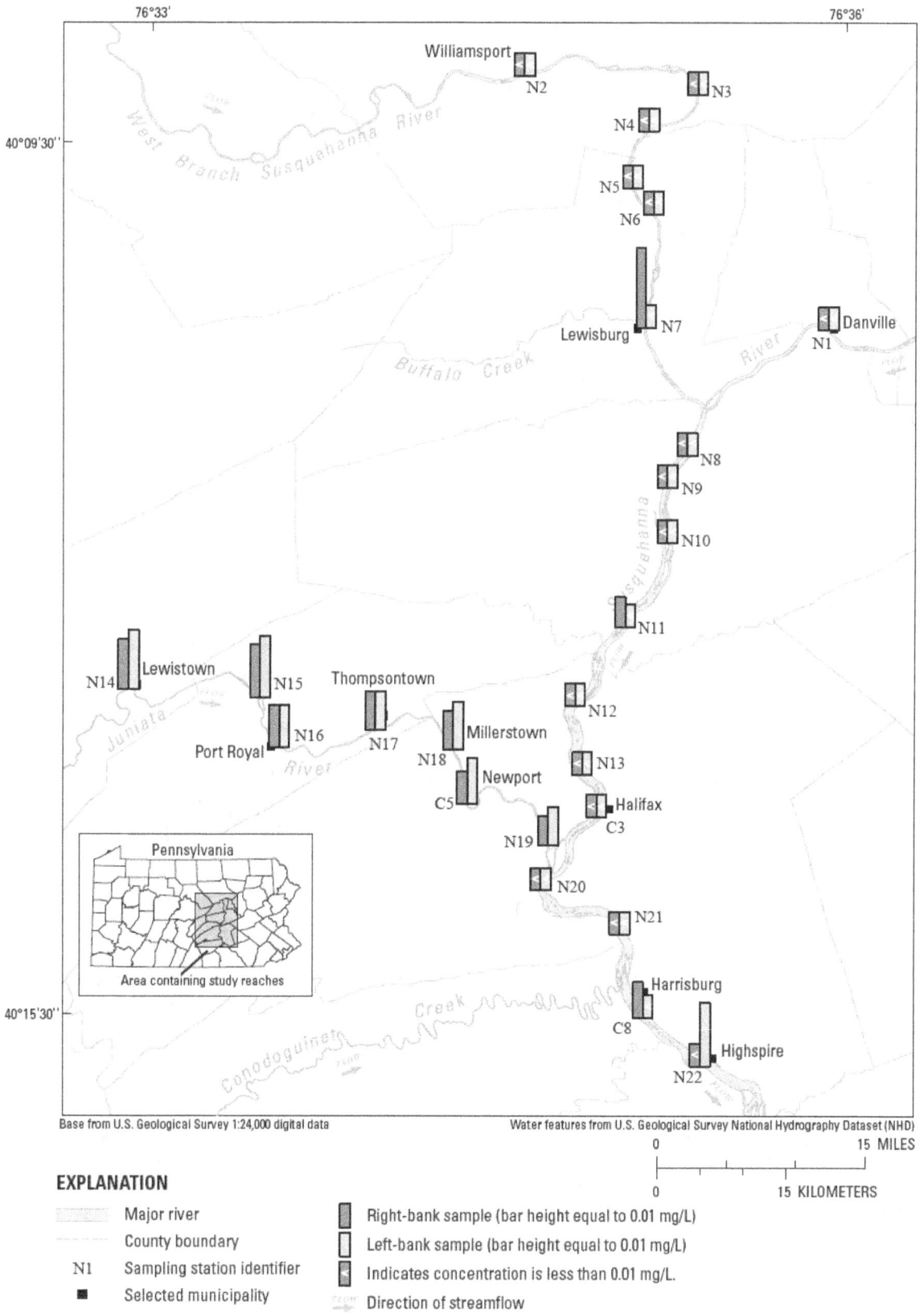

Figure 15. Relative comparison of orthophosphate phosphorus concentrations in water of selected reaches of the Susquehanna River and major tributaries, June 11 and 12, 2008.

As previously stated, this sampling station was likely influenced by inputs from the Conodoguinet Creek (appendix 3, tables 3-1, 3-2, 3-3).

The highest concentration of ammonia plus organic nitrogen, 4.0 g/kg, was measured in sediments from the left-bank sample from the Susquehanna River at Dalmatia (station N11). The second highest, 3.6 g/kg, was in the right-bank sample from the Juniata River at Amity Hall (station N19) (appendix 3, tables 3-1, 3-2, 3-3). No large wastewater effluents are immediately upstream from either of these sampling stations.

Implications of Nutrients in the Susquehanna River

As indicated previously, excessive nutrients in water can spur excessive plant growth leading to dramatic daily swings in dissolved-oxygen concentrations. Previous studies have primarily assessed concentrations of total nitrogen and (or) total phosphorus that are capable of producing nuisance plant growths. The emphasis here is on the word "total." Some studies have looked at algal growth to draw their conclusions (Biggs, 2000; Dodds and others, 2002; Stevenson and others, 2006) and some have looked at the trophic state of the system (Whitmore, 1989; Dodds and others, 1998; Potapova and Charles, 2007; Ponader and others, 2007). Discussions center on whether to set limits using total nitrogen and total phosphorus or their soluble components. Concentrations of total phosphorus attributed to causing excessive growths of algae are between 0.021 and 0.9 mg/L (Dodds and others, 1997; Chetelat and others, 1999; Lohman and others, 1992). Some studies indicate that concentrations of total nitrogen between 0.25 and 0.65 mg/L (Dodds and others, 1997; Lohman and others, 1992) are enough to cause nuisance growths of algae in streams. Sheeder and Evans (2004) calculated concentration thresholds for impaired versus non-impaired watersheds in Pennsylvania. Their analysis established somewhat higher threshold concentrations than other researchers with the threshold for total phosphorus at 0.07 mg/L and for total nitrogen at 2.01 mg/L. Dodds and Welch (2000) recommend that in order to avoid chronic toxicity by ammonia to fish and invertebrates, no more than 0.02 mg/L of ammonia should be present. To date, no consensus limits for phosphorus and nitrogen species in streams and rivers have been reached.

The states have been charged with developing defensible nutrient criteria by EPA. EPA has published recommendations for establishing nutrient criteria by ecoregion. States may adopt the EPA recommended criteria or develop their own. The EPA recommendations are for total nitrogen and total phosphorus. The Susquehanna River Basin is located primarily in nutrient ecoregion XI, the Central and Eastern Forested Uplands, but with portions of the basin in nutrient ecoregions VIII and XI (Commission for Environmental Cooperation, 1997). The area for the current study is almost all in ecoregion XI. For ecoregion XI, the concentration of total phosphorus recommended by EPA is 0.01 mg/L and the concentration of total nitrogen is 0.31 mg/L (U.S. Environmental Protection Agency, 2002). All stations sampled during the June 2008 survey had concentrations of total phosphorus larger than the EPA recommendation to control nuisance algal growth and to promote clean water for ecoregion XI. Similarly, all stations exceeded the recommendation for total nitrogen.

The Commonwealth of Pennsylvania has not yet established water-quality standards for nutrients. However, as of July 2008, 5 states have adopted numeric nutrient standards for one or more constituents for all of their rivers/streams, 9 states have adopted numeric nutrient standards for one or more constituents for part of their rivers/streams, and 36 states have not adopted numeric nutrient standards (U.S. Environmental Protection Agency, 2008). For states that border Pennsylvania, New Jersey has adopted a limit of 0.1 mg/L total phosphorus in streams (Cohen and others, 2009). None of the Susquehanna River stations had a concentration of total phosphorus that exceeded this limit. New York has narrative criteria for nutrients. Delaware has "target" criteria of 0.05 mg/L for total phosphorus and 1.0 mg/L for total nitrogen. Two Susquehanna River Basin stations had concentrations of total phosphorus that exceeded the Delaware target concentration. Applying the Delaware criteria, 22 of the 50 Susquehanna River Basin sampling stations exceeded the target for total nitrogen including all 14 stations on the Juniata River. Maryland, Ohio, and West Virginia have not adopted nutrient criteria for streams.

Concentrations of total phosphorus measured in the study reaches were all in the range considered to be indicative of excessive algal growth. Concentrations of total nitrogen measured in the study reaches routinely exceed the recommendations for controlling nuisance algal growth as recommended by previous studies. The highest nutrient concentrations were measured at stations immediately downstream from wastewater-treatment plants. It should be emphasized that the nutrient survey was conducted during a low-flow period. Nutrient contributions from nonpoint sources would be expected to be at a minimum under these conditions. In general, for all nutrient species, concentrations in the Juniata River were higher than in the West Branch Susquehanna River or in the mainstem Susquehanna River.

Water Quality in 2008 Compared with Available Historical Data

YOY smallmouth-bass mortalities were first recognized in 2005 and continued in 2007 and 2008. Comparison of continuous-monitoring data collected in the Susquehanna River at Harrisburg (station C8) in 2008 with historical data available from the 1970s may indicate if and how temperature and dissolved-oxygen concentrations have changed over time. Further, if growth of periphyton and rooted aquatic plants is contributing to daily oxygen swings, perhaps present-day nutrient concentrations are higher than historic concentrations and are causing that increased growth.

For the Susquehanna River at Harrisburg, Pa., a station that characterizes water quality of the main channel, continuous water-quality data collected by USGS from 1974 to 1979 were compared to water-quality data collected by USGS in 2008. Statistical analyses using the two-sided Wilcoxon signed-rank test indicate daily values for minimum temperature, maximum temperature, temperature range, and mean temperature were all significantly different in the 1970s than in 2008 (table 7). The average daily mean water temperature was 0.8°C warmer (p-value = 0.0056) in 2008 than in the historical record and the average daily mean dissolved-oxygen concentrations was 1.1 mg/L lower (p-value = < 0.0001). These results are consistent with a study that suggests water temperatures in streams in other parts of the world are warming (Webb and Noblis, 2007). Daily mean streamflow was not significantly different between the two time periods (p-value = 0.0952) indicating that it is not a likely explanation for the differences in water quality.

Long-term data indicate that nutrient concentrations are lower presently (2009) than 20 or 30 years ago. This stands to reason because of the large investment that has been made in improving wastewater treatment and the emphasis placed on implementing nonpoint-source best-management practices. A Susquehanna River Basin Commission (SRBC) assessment of trends using flow-adjusted concentrations covering the period

Table 7. Statistical comparison of 2008 and historical (1974–79) water-quality data from the Susquehanna River, Pennsylvania.

[°C, Celsius; µS/cm, microsiemens per centimeter; mg/L, milligrams per liter; ft³/s, cubic feet per second; <, less than; —, too few data to test (N < 20)]

Parameter	Susquehanna River at Harrisburg, historical compared to Susquehanna River at Harrisburg, 2008[1]	
	p-value[2]	N
Minimum water temperature (°C)	0.0132	39
Maximum water temperature (°C)	.0021	39
Water temperature range (°C)	.0083	39
Mean water temperature (°C)	.0056	39
Minimum specific conductance (µS/cm)	< .0001	39
Maximum specific conductance (µS/cm)	< .0001	39
Specific conductance range (µS/cm)	.3145	39
Mean specific conductance (µS/cm)	< .0001	39
Minimum pH (standard units)	—	
Maximum pH (standard units)	—	
pH range (standard units)	—	
Median pH (standard units)	—	
Minimum dissolved oxygen (mg/L)	.0001	20
Maximum dissolved oxygen (mg/L)	< .0001	20
Dissolved oxygen range (mg/L)	.0006	20
Mean dissolved oxygen (mg/L)	< .0001	20
7-day mean minimum dissolved oxygen (mg/L)	—	
7-day mean dissolved oxygen (mg/L)	—	
Mean streamflow (ft³/s)	.0952	92

[1]Results of two-sided Wilcoxon signed-rank test. For historical data, the median of daily mean values computed from May 1–July 31, 1974–79 is used. Only days that had data in all 7 years were included in this analysis. As a result, some parameters could not be tested because there were too few data (N < 20).

[2]For this study, a statistically significant difference exists if the p-value is less than 0.05.

1985 through 2007 (McGonigal, 2008) indicates downward trends in concentrations of most nutrient species at most monitoring stations.

However, analyses of a subset of data from 1998 to 2004 indicates increases in dissolved orthophosphate phosphorus concentrations (for the purpose of this report, dissolved orthophosphate phosphorus will be considered equivalent to dissolved inorganic phosphorus (DIP)). McGonigal (2008) states "[over the past several years there has been] a dramatic increase in dissolved phosphorus and more specifically in dissolved orthophosphate phosphorus. This was apparent during the time period from 1998 to 2004, at all mainstem sites and Newport." For example, the annual mean concentration for DIP in 2007 for the Susquehanna River at Danville was 0.047 mg/L, which is almost three times the long-term mean of 0.018 mg/L for that station (McGonigal, 2008).

Nutrient trends in the Susquehanna River Basin also are analyzed periodically (roughly every 3–5 years) for the Chesapeake Bay Program. Analysis of nutrient data from 1985 through 2004 (Langland and others, 2006) indicates downward trends (0 to 50 percent decrease) in flow-adjusted concentrations of total phosphorus and total nitrogen at all Susquehanna River Basin stations. A recently released summary report updates the trends analyses to include data through 2008 for the Chesapeake Bay tributaries (Langland and others, 2009). This update reaffirms the downward trends in flow-adjusted concentrations of total nitrogen (significant downward trends at all eight stations) and total phosphorus (significant downward trends at seven of eight stations) in the Susquehanna River Basin. However, trends for DIP were significantly upward for five of six stations in the Susquehanna River Basin where DIP was evaluated. These results confirm the observations of recent upward trends in DIP observed by McGonigal (2008).

Periphyton production is known to increase as nutrient concentrations increase (Biggs, 2000; Dodds and others, 2002). The increases in DIP documented by McGonigal (2008) and Langland and others (2009) may have promoted increased periphyton growth over the last few years. If so, then perhaps increased periphyton growth is contributing to stressful levels of dissolved oxygen that could explain why YOY smallmouth bass have only recently been affected by *F. columnare* infections. In summary, it appears that DIP concentrations have increased during the past half decade but the data are not available to evaluate whether these increases lead to *F. columnare* infections in smallmouth bass.

Correlation between Streamflow and Disease Incidence

Because dissolved oxygen and water temperature are suspected to play a role in incidence of *F. columnare* infection, it would be logical to compare water-quality conditions in 2008 with previous years when the disease did (2005 and 2007) and

did not (2006) occur. Unfortunately, continuous monitoring of dissolved oxygen in reaches affected by *F. columnare* infection did not begin until 2008 but streamflow data are available for a much longer period of record. Although streamflow is not a surrogate for dissolved-oxygen concentration or water temperature, some generalizations about the correlation between streamflow and water quality can be made. Relatively high streamflows during summer months, such as those in 2006 (fig. 16A), usually result from runoff that is cooler than the ambient river temperature. Water temperature data collected by SRBC (Andrew Gavin, Susquehanna River Basin Commission, written commun., 2009) in the Susquehanna River approximately 6 mi upstream from station C8 (fig. 6A) at Rockville, Pa., indicate conditions frequently were cooler in May and June 2006 than in the same time period in 2007 (fig. 16B). Stormflows with peaks on June 6 and June 29, 2006, are correlated with an initial decrease in temperature as flow increased, followed by a gradual recovery in water temperature as stormflows receded. As the river water cooled through mixing with the stormwater runoff, dissolved oxygen likely would have increased owing to greater dissolution of oxygen in cool water compared to warm water (fig. 4). In addition, relatively high streamflows commonly increase turbidity, which diminishes penetration of sunlight into the river water. Photosynthesis and respiration by periphyton, algae, and other aquatic vegetation is suppressed with decreasing sunlight causing the amplitude of daily sinusoidal dissolved-oxygen fluctuations to be smaller. For these reasons, relatively high-streamflow conditions and cooler water temperatures in 2006 would promote greater dissolved-oxygen concentrations.

Whether or not water-quality conditions are less stressful to YOY smallmouth bass during relatively high-streamflow summers, streamflow and disease-incidence data indicate that higher streamflows may moderate or eliminate the incidence of *F. columnare* infection in YOY smallmouth bass. No *F. columnare* infections were documented in 2006, a year with relatively high spring and summertime streamflows, but YOY smallmouth-bass mortalities were widespread in years 2005, 2007, and 2008 (fig. 17) when flows during the critical period were lower. Summertime months of 2008 had conditions similar to 2005 and 2007, with streamflows that generally are closer to historical median flows than minimum flows for the period of record (fig. 18B and C). Thus, the occurrence of the disease does not seem to be limited to exceptionally low streamflow summers. Moderate or near-normal summertime streamflows and associated water-quality conditions seem to be conducive to widespread occurrence of *F. columnare* infection.

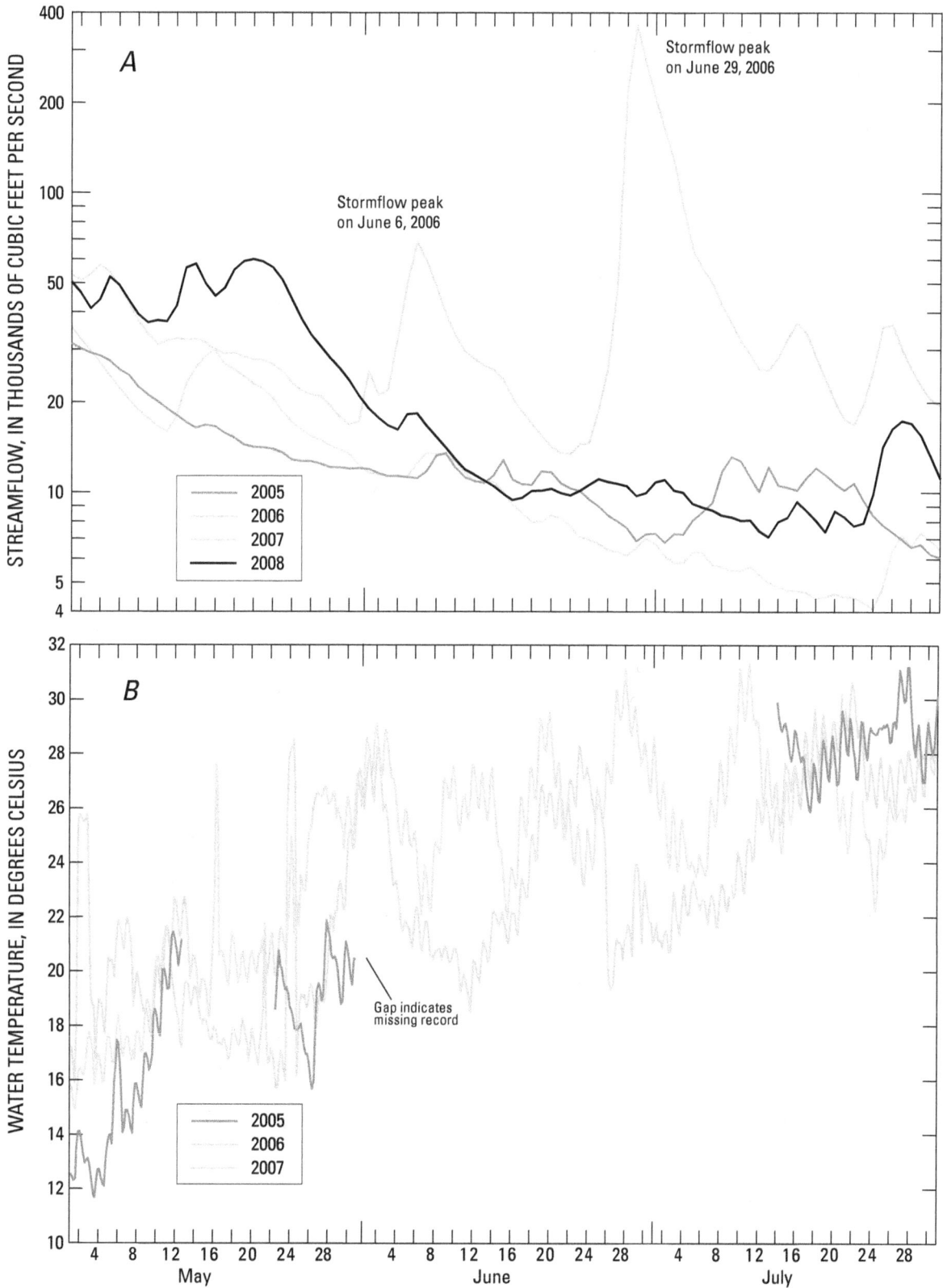

Figure 16.   Relation between *A*) streamflows in the Susquehanna River at Harrisburg, Pennsylvania (station C8), and *B*) water temperature measured approximately 6 miles upstream at Rockville, Pennsylvania, 2005–08.
[Water temperature data provided by Susquehanna River Basin Commission]

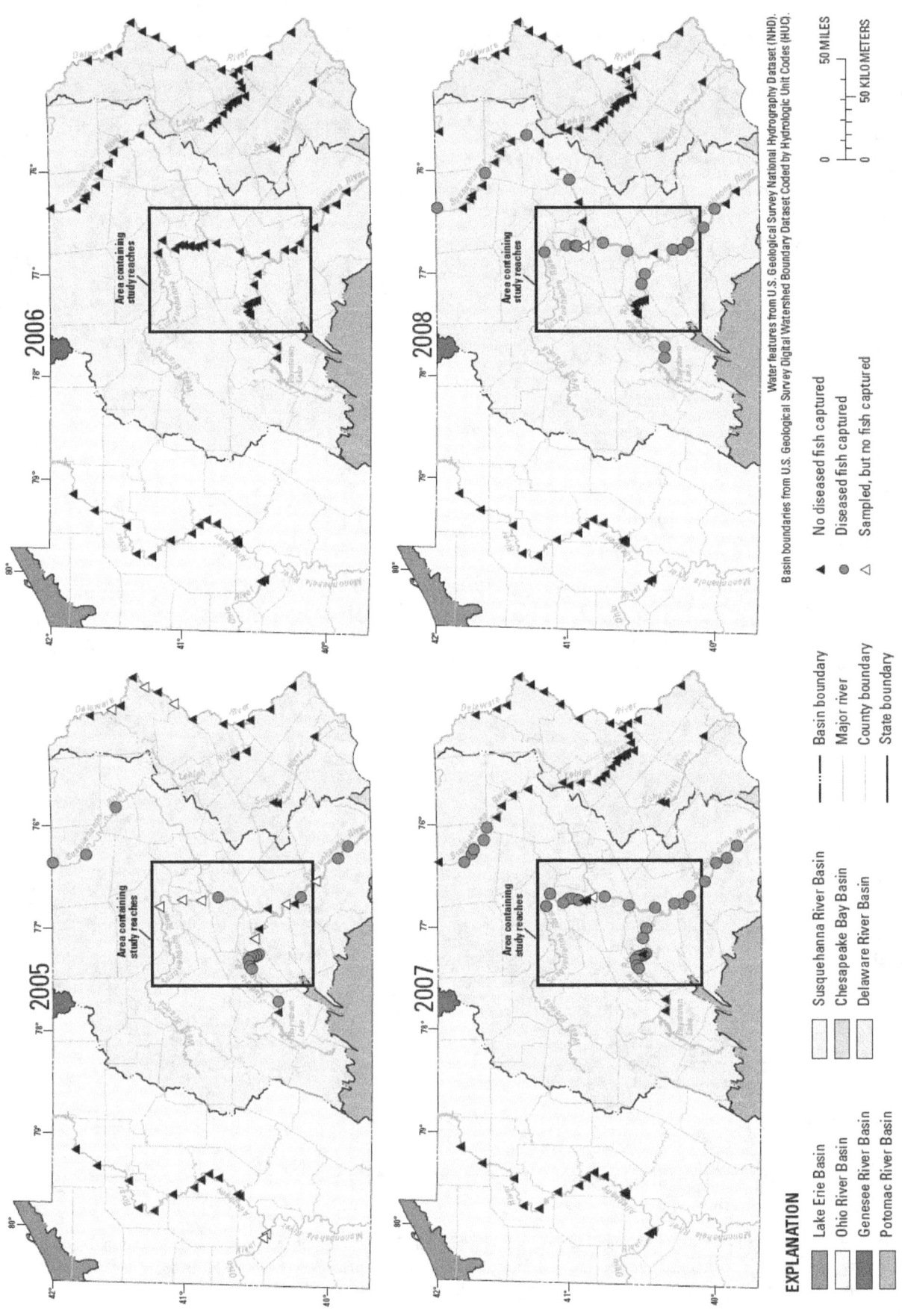

Figure 17.   Geographic distribution of disease incidence in 2008 compared to 2005–07, Pennsylvania.

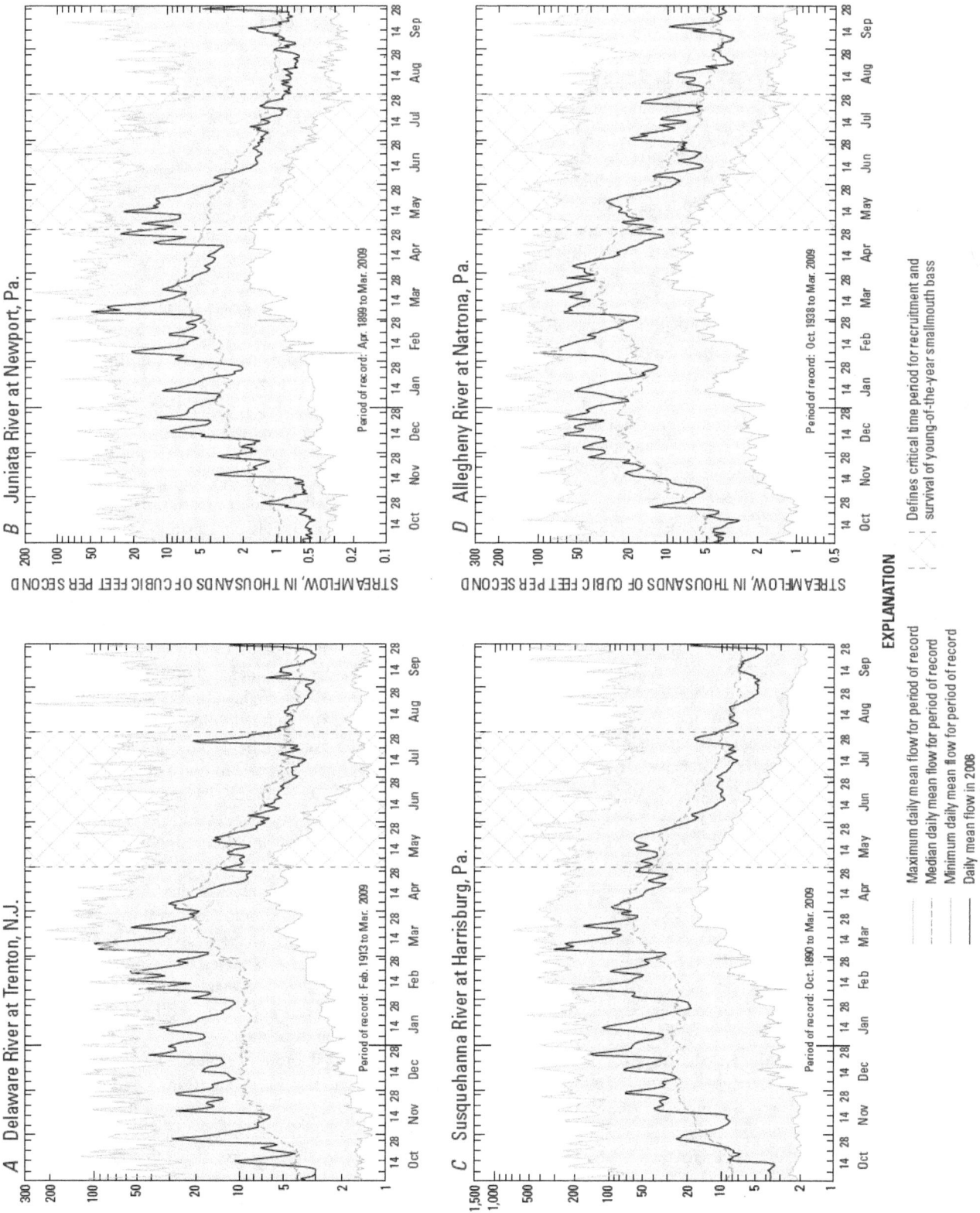

Figure 18.   Relation between 2008 streamflow and historical streamflow at selected streamgages in Pennsylvania and New Jersey.

Water-Quality Differences among the Susquehanna, Delaware, and Allegheny Rivers

In Pennsylvania, infection of YOY smallmouth bass by *F. columnare* has been documented through annual surveys by PFBC biologists in the mainstem of the Susquehanna River and major tributaries including the Juniata River and the West Branch Susquehanna River. Collections of fish for development of an index of biotic integrity in Pennsylvania streams indicate YOY smallmouth bass in smaller tributaries to the Susquehanna River may also be afflicted (Douglas Fischer, Pennsylvania Fish and Boat Commission, written commun., 2009). At this time (2009), no incidents of bacterial infection have been reported in the Delaware River Basin to the east or the Allegheny River Basin to the west (fig. 17). The objective of this section is to compare water temperature, dissolved oxygen, and pH collected in the Susquehanna River at Harrisburg (station C8) with corresponding data from the Delaware River at Trenton, N.J. (station C1) and the Allegheny River at Acmetonia, Pa. (station C10). In addition, a discussion of the possible role of emerging contaminants (contaminants not commonly monitored, but recently detected in the environment) is provided.

If dissolved-oxygen concentrations and water temperatures are indicative of more stressful conditions in the Susquehanna River compared to the Delaware or Allegheny Rivers, this may be viewed as evidence that they play a role in predisposing YOY smallmouth bass to infection by *F. columnare*. However, there are many other pathogens (viral and bacterial) and water-quality stressors like pharmaceutical and pesticide contaminants that were not investigated in this study but may be larger factors in fish diseases in the Susquehanna River compared to the Delaware or Allegheny Rivers. In addition, there are differences in management of water quantity among the three rivers, including how stored water is released from reservoirs, that may influence water quality and factor into the incidence of infection by *F. columnare*.

Daily range in dissolved-oxygen concentration was similar in the Susquehanna River at Harrisburg (station C8) and the Delaware River at Trenton (station C1) (mean daily ranges of 2.3 and 2.4 mg/L) but appreciably lower in the Allegheny River at Acmetonia (station C10) (mean daily range of only 0.5 mg/L, table 8). This indicates the sinusoidal daily fluctuations in the Allegheny River were suppressed compared to the Susquehanna and Delaware Rivers. As a result, daily mean dissolved-oxygen concentrations in the Allegheny River were only slightly greater than in the Susquehanna River (average daily means were 7.9 mg/L compared to 7.6 mg/L; p-value = 0.0624, table 9) even though daily minimum dissolved-oxygen concentrations were consistently lower in the Susquehanna River than in the Allegheny River (fig. 19C).

Daily minimum dissolved-oxygen concentrations were lower than the national criterion for protecting earlylife stages of warm-water fish (5.0 mg/L) on 6 days during the critical period in the Susquehanna River at Harrisburg (station C8) but did not drop below this criterion in the Delaware River at Trenton or the Allegheny River at Acmetonia. Seven-day mean dissolved-oxygen concentrations did not fall below the national criterion at any of the three stations (fig. 20) but were appreciably lower in the Susquehanna River at station C8 and Allegheny River at station C10 (average values of 7.5 mg/L at station C8 and 7.9 mg/L at station C10; appendix 2) compared to the Delaware River at station C1 (average value of 9.1 mg/L).

During the critical period, average daily mean water temperature in the Susquehanna River at station C8 was 1.8°C warmer than in the Delaware River at station C1 and 3.4°C warmer than in the Allegheny River at station C10 (table 8). Daily minimum water temperature was similar (p-value = 0.0709) between stations C8 and C1 (fig. 19A) but the average was 2.6°C warmer at station C8 than at station C10 (p-value = 0.0102). These results indicate that stress induced by sub-optimal dissolved-oxygen conditions is likely to be magnified by elevated temperature in the Susquehanna River at station C8 compared to the Delaware River at station C1 or the Allegheny River at station C10.

The pH of the Susquehanna River at station C8 during the critical period typically was less than the Delaware River at station C1 (median daily median was 0.6 pH units lower) but greater than the Allegheny River at station C10 (median daily median was 0.8 pH units greater) (table 8) and was well within the tolerance limits for smallmouth bass (Cooper and Wagner, 1973). Although the daily maximum, minimum, and median pH values in the Susquehanna River station C8 are all statistically different compared to stations on the Allegheny and Delaware Rivers (p-values < 0.0001), the biological significance of these differences has not been tested. Other research indicates that sustained alkaline pH can disrupt ion balance and ammonia excretion in perch, but despite this stress these fish are not inclined to move to more neutral water (Scott and others, 2005). YOY smallmouth bass in the Delaware River were exposed to the highest pH during the critical period (maximum pH = 9.4; table 8) and commonly experienced pH that exceeded 9.0 (fig. 19E and F) yet *F. columnare* infections are prevalent in the lower pH waters of the Susquehanna River but have not been documented in the Delaware River. If the infections were brought on by stress from alkaline pH alone the Delaware River would be expected to have greater incidence of infection than the Susquehanna River. Other potential stressors such as concentration of carbon dioxide have not been studied but may be important.

Speculation about the role of emerging contaminants in aquatic systems is growing. Some emerging contaminants can act as endocrine disruptors (chemicals having the potential to affect hormonal processes, such as reproduction or immune responses [Glassmeyer, 2007]). This disruption can affect the immune system of fish, making them more susceptible to disease and bacterial infections (Robertson and others, 2009). An ongoing joint effort between the USGS and PADEP

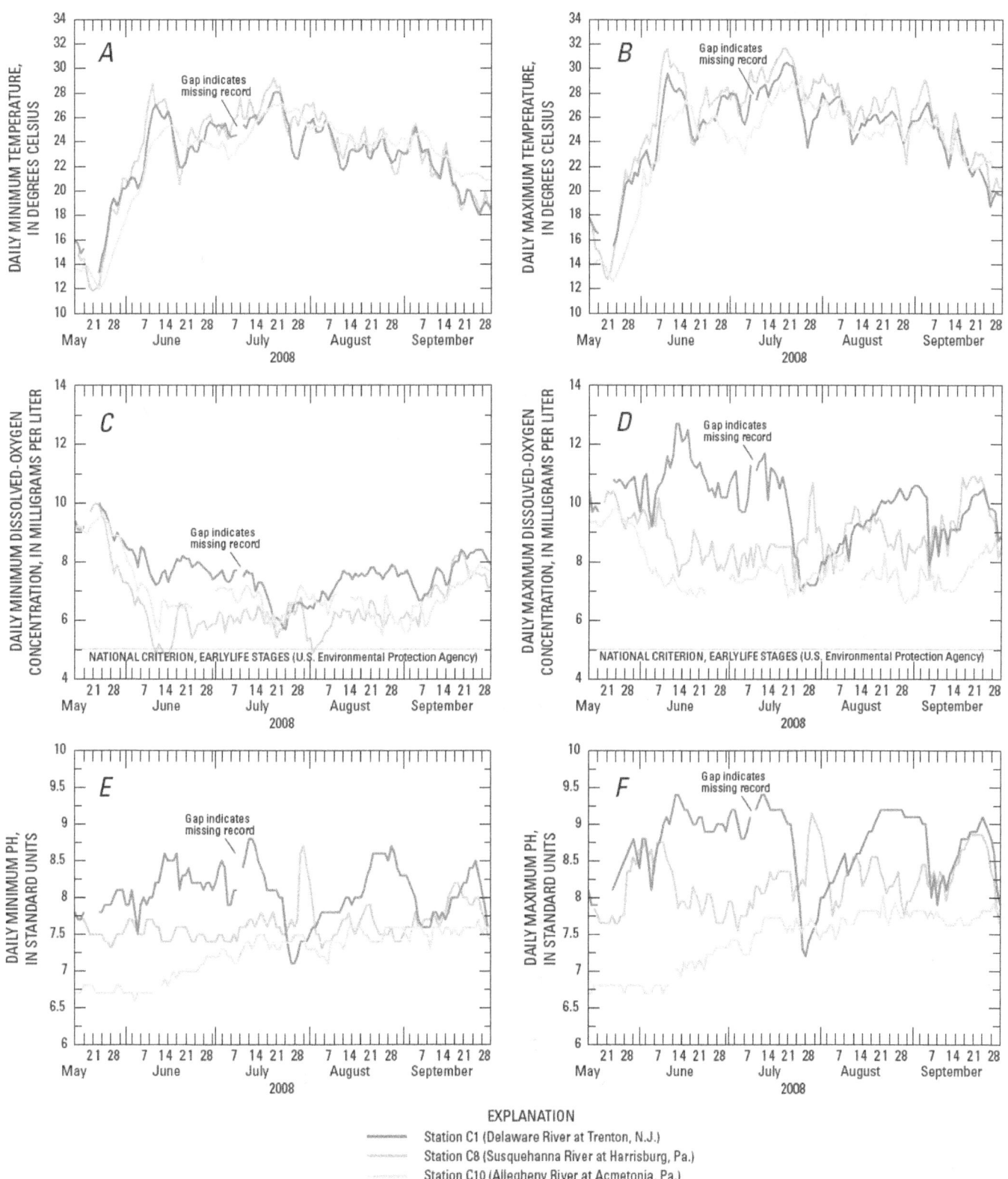

EXPLANATION

——— Station C1 (Delaware River at Trenton, N.J.)
········ Station C8 (Susquehanna River at Harrisburg, Pa.)
········ Station C10 (Allegheny River at Acmetonia, Pa.)

Figure 19. Comparison of water quality in the Susquehanna River at Harrisburg, Pennsylvania, Delaware River at Trenton, New Jersey, and Allegheny River at Acmetonia, Pennsylvania, 2008.

Table 8. Summary statistics for water-quality data collected in the Delaware River at Trenton, New Jersey, Susquehanna River at Harrisburg, Pennsylvania, and the Allegheny River at Acmetonia, Pennsylvania, 2008.

[C1, Delaware River at Trenton, N.J.; C8, Susquehanna River at Harrisburg, Pa.; C10, Allegheny River at Lock and Dam 3 at Acmetonia, Pa.; C, degrees Celsius; mg/L, milligrams per liter; µS/cm, microsiemens per centimeter; n, number of daily values; P25, 25th percentile; P75, 75th percentile]

Statistic	Daily minimum temperature (°C) Station			Daily mean temperature (°C) Station			Daily maximum temperature (°C) Station			Daily temperature range (°C) Station		
	C1	C8	C10	C1	C8	C10	C1	C8	C10	C1	C8	C10
n	87	77	92	87	77	92	87	77	92	87	77	92
Minimum	12.8	11.8	12.0	13.9	12.2	12.3	14.3	12.8	12.6	.6	.6	.1
P25	18.0	21.7	15.0	18.8	23.0	15.2	19.9	23.9	15.6	1.6	2.1	.7
Median	23.4	25.2	23.5	24.5	26.3	23.9	25.5	27.5	24.4	2.0	2.7	1.0
P75	25.5	26.4	24.9	26.7	28.0	25.4	27.9	29.6	26.4	2.5	3.2	1.5
Maximum	28.1	29.2	27.1	29.2	30.3	27.7	30.5	31.7	29.5	3.4	4.1	3.3
Mean	21.8	23.4	20.8	22.8	24.6	21.2	23.8	26.0	22.0	2.0	2.6	1.1
Standard deviation	4.7	4.7	5.1	4.8	4.9	5.2	5.0	5.0	5.5	.7	.8	.6

Statistic	Daily minimum dissolved oxygen (mg/L) Station			Daily mean dissolved oxygen (mg/L) Station			Daily maximum dissolved oxygen (mg/L) Station			Daily dissolved oxygen range (mg/L) Station		
	C1	C8	C10	C1	C8	C10	C1	C8	C10	C1	C8	C10
n	87	73	85	87	73	85	87	73	85	87	73	85
Minimum	5.7	4.8	5.6	6.6	6.1	6.4	7.0	7.3	6.8	.5	.3	.1
P25	7.4	5.9	6.6	8.9	6.9	7.0	9.9	8.2	7.3	1.3	2.0	.3
Median	7.8	6.1	7.1	9.3	7.4	7.3	10.7	8.6	7.7	2.4	2.3	.4
P75	8.8	6.6	9.0	9.7	8.1	9.1	11.2	9.4	9.3	3.4	2.7	.6
Maximum	10.0	10.0	9.6	11.0	10.2	9.7	12.7	10.7	9.8	5.1	3.9	2.1
Mean	8.0	6.5	7.6	9.2	7.6	7.9	10.4	8.8	8.1	2.4	2.3	.5
Standard deviation	1.1	1.2	1.2	1.0	.9	1.1	1.3	.8	1.0	1.3	.8	.4

Table 8. Summary statistics for water-quality data collected in the Delaware River at Trenton, New Jersey, Susquehanna River at Harrisburg, Pennsylvania, and the Allegheny River at Acmetonia, Pennsylvania, 2008.—Continued

[C1, Delaware River at Trenton, N.J.; C8, Susquehanna River at Harrisburg, Pa.; C10, Allegheny River at Lock and Dam 3 at Acmetonia, Pa.; C, degrees Celsius; mg/L, milligrams per liter; μS/cm, microsiemens per centimeter; n, number of daily values; P25, 25th percentile; P75, 75th percentile]

Statistic	Daily minimum pH (standard units)			Daily median pH (standard units)			Daily maximum pH (standard units)			Daily pH Range (standard units)		
	Station			**Station**			**Station**			**Station**		
	C1	C8	C10	C1	C8	C10	C1	C8	C10	C1	C8	C10
n	87	76	91	87	76	91	87	76	91	87	76	91
Minimum	7.1	7.3	6.6	7.2	7.5	6.7	7.2	7.6	6.7	.1	.1	.0
P25	7.8	7.5	6.7	8.0	7.6	6.8	8.3	7.8	6.8	.5	.4	.1
Median	8.0	7.5	6.9	8.4	7.8	7.0	8.8	8.1	7.0	.7	.6	.1
P75	8.2	7.6	7.3	8.8	8.0	7.4	9.1	8.4	7.4	.8	.8	.2
Maximum	8.8	8.7	7.5	9.2	8.9	7.6	9.4	9.2	7.7	1.1	1.3	.4
Mean	8.0	7.6	7.0	8.4	7.9	7.1	8.7	8.2	7.1	.6	.6	.1
Standard deviation	.4	.2	.3	.5	.3	.3	.6	.4	.3	.3	.3	.1

Statistic	Daily minimum specific conductance (μS/cm)			Daily mean specific conductance (μS/cm)			Daily maximum specific conductance (μS/cm)			Daily specific conductance range (μS/cm)		
	Station			**Station**			**Station**			**Station**		
	C1	C8	C10	C1	C8	C10	C1	C8	C10	C1	C8	C10
n	87	77	92	87	77	92	87	77	92	87	77	92
Minimum	105	142	214	110	144	220	118	146	224	2	1	2
P25	198	194	241	204	199	248	209	205	255	5	7	8
Median	217	273	264	222	279	271	227	285	283	7	10	11
P75	234	293	296	239	298	301	245	303	306	11	15	16
Maximum	254	349	361	261	352	367	266	356	375	123	47	64
Mean	212	248	269	218	254	276	223	260	283	11	12	14
Standard deviation	32	59	35	30	60	36	29	61	38	14	8	11

Table 9.   Statistical comparison of water quality in the Susquehanna River at Harrisburg, Pennsylvania, to water quality in the Delaware River at Trenton, New Jersey, and the Allegheny River at Acmetonia, Pennsylvania, 2008.

[°C, Celsius; μS/cm, microsiemens per centimeter; mg/L, milligrams per liter; <, less than]

Constituent	p-value[1]	
	Susquehanna River at Harrisburg compared to Delaware River at Trenton[2]	Susquehanna River at Harrisburg compared to Allegheny River at Acmetonia[2]
Minimum water temperature (°C)	0.0709	0.0102
Maximum water temperature (°C)	.0104	< .0001
Water temperature range (°C)	< .0001	< .0001
Mean water temperature (°C)	.0276	.0001
Minimum specific conductance (μS/cm)	< .0001	.0504
Maximum specific conductance (μS/cm)	< .0001	.0304
Specific conductance range (μS/cm)	.0493	.3196
Mean specific conductance (μS/cm)	< .0001	.0408
Minimum pH (standard units)	< .0001	< .0001
Maximum pH (standard units)	< .0001	< .0001
pH range (standard units)	.0360	< .0001
Median pH (standard units)	< .0001	< .0001
Minimum dissolved oxygen (mg/L)	< .0001	< .0001
Maximum dissolved oxygen (mg/L)	< .0001	< .0001
Dissolved oxygen range (mg/L)	.0406	< .0001
Mean dissolved oxygen (mg/L)	< .0001	.0624
7-day mean minimum dissolved oxygen (mg/L)	< .0001	< .0001
7-day mean dissolved oxygen (mg/L)	< .0001	.0631

[1]For this study, a statistically significant difference exists if the p-value is less than 0.05.

[2]Results of two-sided Wilcoxon rank-sum test.

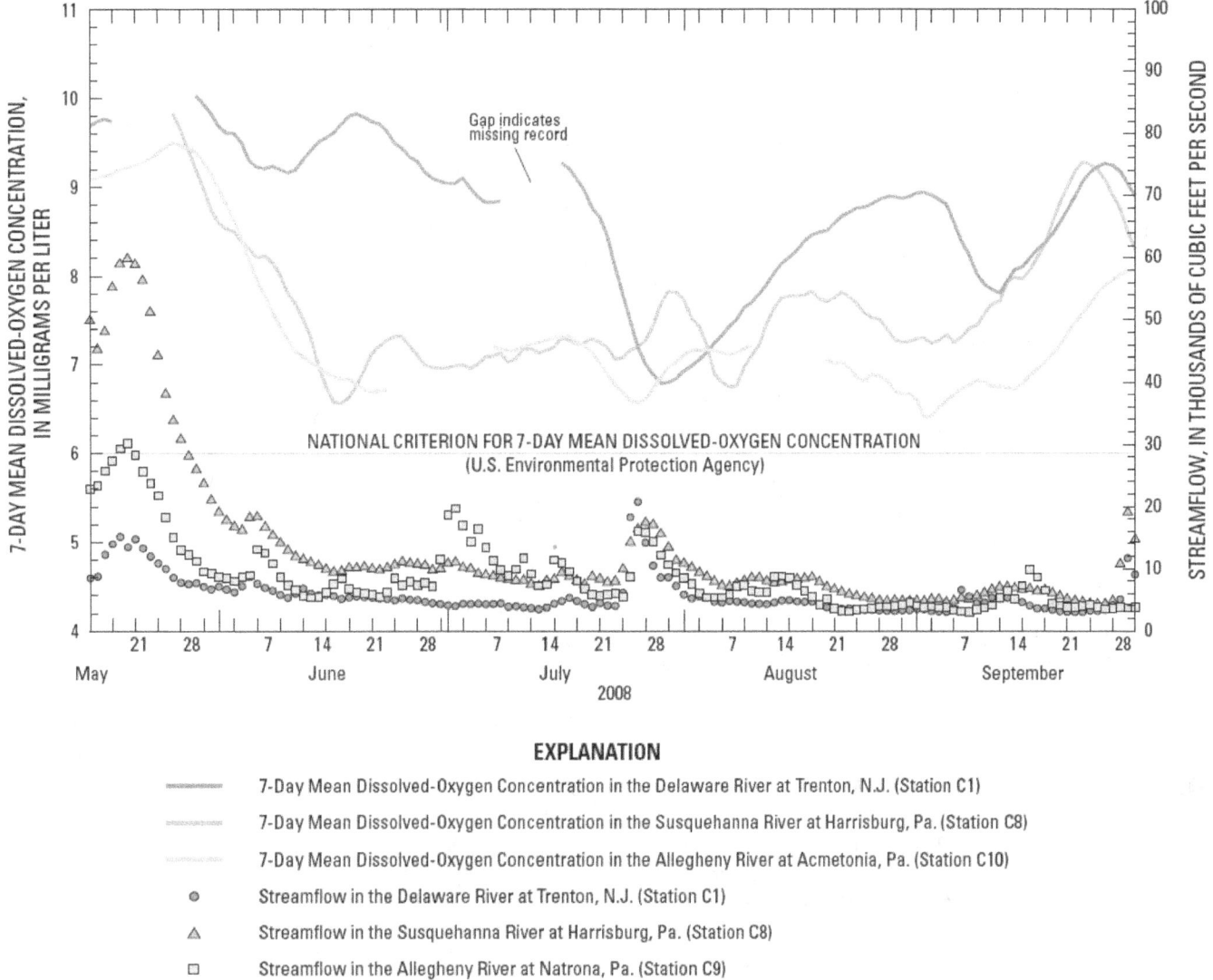

EXPLANATION

———	7-Day Mean Dissolved-Oxygen Concentration in the Delaware River at Trenton, N.J. (Station C1)
———	7-Day Mean Dissolved-Oxygen Concentration in the Susquehanna River at Harrisburg, Pa. (Station C8)
———	7-Day Mean Dissolved-Oxygen Concentration in the Allegheny River at Acmetonia, Pa. (Station C10)
⊙	Streamflow in the Delaware River at Trenton, N.J. (Station C1)
△	Streamflow in the Susquehanna River at Harrisburg, Pa. (Station C8)
□	Streamflow in the Allegheny River at Natrona, Pa. (Station C9)

Figure 20. Seven-day mean dissolved-oxygen concentration and streamflow conditions in the Susquehanna River at Harrisburg, Pennsylvania, Delaware River at Trenton, New Jersey, and Allegheny River at Acmetonia, Pennsylvania, 2008. [Steamflow data are not available for the Allegheny River at Acmetonia, Pennsylvania. Therefore, hydrologic conditions for this station are represented by streamflow measured at Natrona, Pennsylvania (Station C9), which is located approximately 9.75 mi upstream.]

measured antibiotics, pharmaceutical compounds, hormones, and wastewater compounds at two locations in the Susquehanna River in 2007. These locations are the Susquehanna River at Danville, Pa., and the Susquehanna River at Wolverton, Pa. (approximately 4.7 mi upstream from the confluence with the West Branch Susquehanna River). These sampling stations were selected to be upstream and downstream of the municipal wastewater discharge from Danville, Pa. Similar sampling was conducted at limited locations in the Delaware River Basin and the Ohio River Basin. Coincident with the water-quality sampling, smallmouth bass were captured and examined for incidence of intersex, the presence of oocytes (immature ova or egg cells) within the testes of male fishes. The intersex condition was common in smallmouth bass from the Susquehanna River but not in smallmouth bass from the Delaware or Ohio River Basins (Blazer and others, 2009). It is not clear whether the incidence of intersex in smallmouth bass and the *F. columnare* infections are related. Further, it is not clear whether the very low concentrations (typically less than 1 µg/L) of emerging contaminants measured in samples from the Susquehanna River contribute to the prevalence of intersex. Additional studies would be needed to more clearly define any associations. The USGS, in cooperation with PFBC and PADEP, is conducting a pilot study in 2009 to investigate the issue.

Summary and Conclusions

In the summer of 2005, Pennsylvania Fish and Boat Commission fisheries biologists discovered an unusually high number of the young-of-the-year (YOY) smallmouth bass (*Micropterus dolomieu*) in the mainstem of the Susquehanna River, West Branch Susquehanna River, and Juniata River (affected reaches) infected by *Flavobacterium columnare*, a ubiquitous bacterium common in soil and water. No YOY smallmouth bass captured during 2005 surveys in the Delaware or Allegheny River Basins were infected. In the summer months of 2006, which had relatively high streamflows compared to 2005, no *F. columnare* infections were observed in Pennsylvania streams, but the disease returned to affected reaches of the Susquehanna River Basin in 2007 when streamflow was measured at lower levels. After the disease and subsequent mortalities were discovered, reconnaissance efforts by Pennsylvania Fish and Boat Commission biologists documented concentrations of dissolved oxygen in the Susquehanna River that were stressful (below 5.0 mg/L, the national criterion for protecting earlylife stages of warm-water fish). Adequate concentrations of dissolved oxygen are especially important for proper development and survival of YOY smallmouth bass because the young bass require more dissolved oxygen than more mature fish. After hatching, the young spend the critical period (defined for this study as May 1 through July 31) in the same habitat where they were born.

In response to the YOY smallmouth bass mortalities, the U.S. Geological Survey, in cooperation with the Pennsylvania Fish and Boat Commission, Pennsylvania Department of Environmental Protection, and PPL Corporation, conducted a study from May through October 2008 to assess dissolved oxygen, temperature, pH, and specific conductance in reaches of the Susquehanna River and major tributaries that represent affected reaches within the basin. Water-quality data were collected between May and October 2008 by continuous (30-minute interval) water-quality meters (sondes). Four sondes were deployed as pairs to evaluate differences between main-channel habitats and YOY smallmouth-bass microhabitats (habitat of YOY smallmouth bass) on the Susquehanna River and Juniata River. Two additional sondes were collocated with streamgages at Harrisburg and Newport, Pa. Historical water-quality and streamflow data at Harrisburg allowed for comparison with 2008 conditions. Discrete samples for nitrogen and phosphorus in water and streambed sediment were also collected on June 11 and 12, 2008, to determine concentrations at 25 locations in the Susquehanna River and tributaries between Williamsport and Highspire, Pa.

Daily minimum dissolved-oxygen concentration at microhabitats in the Susquehanna River at Clemson Island (station C4) and the Juniata River at Howe Township Park (station C6) generally were lower than nearby main-channel habitats indicating YOY smallmouth bass are exposed to more stressful conditions than adult fish occupying habitat outside of microhabitat areas. Average daily minimum dissolved-oxygen concentrations at C4 and C6 were significantly lower (1.1 and 0.3 mg/L, respectively) than in the corresponding main-channel habitat during the critical period. The lowest dissolved-oxygen concentrations in the microhabitats during the critical period were 3.3 mg/L at station C4 (June 11, 2008) and 4.1 mg/L at station C6 (July 22, 2008).

The 7-day mean dissolved-oxygen concentrations at all stations remained above the 6.0 mg/L national criterion for protecting earlylife stages of warm-water fish, but daily minimum dissolved-oxygen concentrations in both microhabitats and in the Juniata River main-channel habitat sometimes were lower than the national criterion (5.0 mg/L) during nighttime and early-morning hours (midnight to 0800). For example, during the critical period, daily minimum dissolved-oxygen concentrations in the Susquehanna River at station C4 were lower than 5.0 mg/L on 31 out of 92 days compared to no days in the main-channel habitat at station C3. In the Juniata River, daily minimum dissolved-oxygen concentration in the microhabitat at station C6 was lower than 5.0 mg/L on 20 days compared to only 5 days in the main channel. The maximum time periods that dissolved oxygen was less than 5.0 mg/L in microhabitats of the Susquehanna and Juniata Rivers were 8.5 and 5.5 hours, respectively. These data support the contention that YOY smallmouth bass in the study reaches are more likely to experience stress from sub-optimal dissolved-oxygen concentrations than older fish not living in or frequenting microhabitat.

Microhabitats did not uniformly have warmer water temperatures and are, therefore, not necessarily more stressful than main-channel habitats solely because of water temperature. Site-specific variables like exposure to sunlight may have factored greatly in the measured differences between microhabitats in the Susquehanna and Juniata Rivers. The microhabitat in the Susquehanna River at station C4 had minimum, median, and maximum daily water temperatures comparable to the main channel at station C3, which received similar exposure to sun. Mean daily water temperatures had medians of 25.8°C at station C4 and 26.1°C at station C3 and maximum daily water temperatures had medians of 28.5°C at C4 compared to 28.4°C at C3. By contrast, the microhabitat in the Juniata River at station C6 had significantly cooler water temperatures compared to the main channel owing to shade from a canopy of trees. Daily maximum water temperature in the microhabitat at station C6 had a median of 26.9°C compared to 27.8°C in the main-channel habitat.

During the critical period, pH for microhabitat and main-channel stations in the Susquehanna River at Clemson Island and Juniata River at Howe Township Park ranged from 7.2 to 9.4 and had a daily change of as much as 1.6 units. YOY smallmouth bass are sensitive to acidic pH and experience appreciable declines in survival rates at pH 5.7 and below, but the primary concern for this study was exposure to alkaline (greater than 9.0) pH. For stations in microhabitats of the Susquehanna and Juniata Rivers, daily pH minima, maxima, and medians generally were up to 0.5 pH units lower than in the main-channel habitats. Despite significant statistical differences between pH of the microhabitats and main-channel habitats, the biological significance is unclear. YOY smallmouth bass rarely were exposed to pH that exceeded 9.0 during the critical period, and values this high were sustained for periods of less than 12 hours. It therefore seems unlikely that pH is a major stressor to YOY smallmouth bass in the study reaches, but perhaps when combined with temperatures that are relatively high and dissolved-oxygen concentrations that are below national criteria, alkaline pH and (or) large daily fluctuations in pH may contribute to overall stress.

Susquehanna River streamflow conditions during the critical period of 2008 were similar to those in 2005 and 2007 when the disease previously occurred. As in 2005 and 2007, mortality of YOY smallmouth bass throughout the affected reaches was prevalent. Streamflow during the critical period of 2008 (or 2005 and 2007) was not extremely low when compared to historical streamflows. Instead, streamflow was comparable to or slightly lower than historical medians. Thus, the occurrence of the disease does not seem to be limited to exceptionally low streamflow summers. Moderate or near-normal summertime streamflows and associated water-quality conditions seem to be conducive to widespread occurrence of *F. columnare* infection.

Dissolved-oxygen data indicate stressful conditions existed more often at stations in the Susquehanna River than in the Delaware or Allegheny Rivers. Daily minimum dissolved-oxygen concentrations were lower than the national criterion

for protecting earlylife stages of warm-water fish (5.0 mg/L) on 6 days during the critical period in the Susquehanna River at Harrisburg (station C8) but did not drop below this criterion in the Delaware River at Trenton or the Allegheny River at Acmetonia. The 7-day mean dissolved-oxygen concentrations did not fall below the national criterion at any of the three stations, but the 7-day mean dissolved-oxygen concentration was appreciably lower in the Susquehanna River at station C8 and in the Allegheny River at station C10 than in the Delaware River at Trenton. On average, 7-day mean dissolved-oxygen concentrations during the critical period were 7.5 mg/L at station C8 and 7.9 mg/L at station C10 compared to 9.1 mg/L at station C1 in the Delaware River. More stressful conditions (lower dissolved oxygen accompanied by higher water temperature) in the Susquehanna River compared to the Delaware or Allegheny Rivers may be viewed as evidence that environmental factors such as dissolved oxygen and water temperature play a role in predisposing YOY smallmouth bass to colonization by *F. columnare*. However, many other water-quality factors (pharmaceutical and pesticide contaminants, for example) and pathogens (viral and bacterial) were not investigated in this study and may contribute to fish diseases in the Susquehanna River more than in the Delaware or Allegheny Rivers.

The average daily mean water temperature in the Susquehanna River at station C8 was 1.8°C warmer than in the Delaware River at station C1 and 3.4°C warmer than in the Allegheny River at station C10. These results indicate that stress induced by sub-optimal dissolved-oxygen conditions is likely to be magnified by elevated temperature in the Susquehanna River station C8 compared to the Delaware River at station C1 or the Allegheny River at station C10.

Concentrations of total phosphorus and total nitrogen measured in water from the Susquehanna River and its tributaries were routinely within the range considered to be conducive to excessive algal growth, based on previous studies. The highest nutrient concentrations were measured at stations immediately downstream from wastewater-treatment plants. In general, for all nutrient species, concentrations in the Juniata River were higher than in the West Branch Susquehanna River or in the mainstem Susquehanna River. Concentrations of nutrients in streambed-sediment samples were variable suggesting these concentrations may have been more dependent on the sediment grain size rather than on the nutrient regime of the sampling location. As a result, the streambed-sediment analyses were inconclusive.

Statistical analyses using the two-sided Wilcoxon signed-rank test indicate minimum temperature, maximum temperature, temperature range, and mean temperature were all significantly different during the critical period in 2008 compared to a historical dataset from 1974 to 1979. The average daily mean water temperature was 0.8°C warmer in 2008 compared to the available historical data. Dissolved-oxygen concentrations were significantly lower in 2008 compared to the available historical data. Streamflow was not significantly different between the two time periods indicating that it is not a likely explanation for the differences in water temperature or dissolved oxygen.

In summary, the data collected during this study indicate 1) microhabitats where YOY smallmouth bass live were more stressful, based on measured water-quality conditions, than nearby main-channel habitats; 2) dissolved-oxygen concentrations and water temperatures in the Susquehanna River were more stressful in 2008 than in the 1970s; 3) moderate or near-normal and lower summertime streamflows and associated water-quality conditions seem to be conducive to widespread occurrence of *F. columnare* infection; and 4) dissolved-oxygen concentrations and water temperatures during this study were more stressful for YOY smallmouth bass in the Susquehanna River than in the Delaware or Allegheny Rivers. Although the YOY smallmouth bass mortalities cannot be linked to any one water-quality factor or environmental condition on the basis of this study, the results from this study and ongoing investigations of other pathogens (viral and bacterial) and water-quality stressors (like pharmaceutical and pesticide contaminants) could be used as a foundation for a long-term network of data collection and interpretation.

Acknowledgments

The cooperation, guidance, and support of the PFBC are gratefully acknowledged. John Arway served as the study director for the PFBC during the study and contributed his scientific expertise, ideas, and coordination skills to help make the project successful. John Frederick of the PFBC contributed his time and skill as a boat operator to the project. Robert Lorantas, Kris Kuhn, Leroy Young, and Karl Stephan of the PFBC are also acknowledged for their contributions to this study. Numerous individuals in the PADEP are recognized for their contributions, including: Richard Shertzer, Robert Schott, Joseph Hepp, Martin Friday, Kristen Bardell, Jay Gerber, and Michael Lookenbill. Staff from the SRBC, including David Heicher, Jennifer Hoffman, Andrew Gavin, and Susan Obleski, also are recognized for their contributions to this study. Linda Zarr, Joanne Irvin, and David Smith of the USGS assisted with the data compilation, data management, and graphics-presentation tasks. Mark Beaver (USGS) offered insight on sonde placement and deployment. David O'Brien (USGS) provided boat operation support. Kim Otto of the USGS provided valuable support and guidance in report preparation. USGS reviewers John Clune, Douglas Chambers, Robert Hainly, and Kevin Breen along with John Arway of PFBC, Joseph Hepp of PADEP, and Nancy Evans of PPL Corporation offered valuable suggestions for improving the report. Finally, we acknowledge Anthony Trease of the USGS for being the primary data-collection technician and Michael Burton of the Pennsylvania Bass Federation for volunteering his time, equipment, and boating expertise. To all who helped in any way, the authors thank you.

References Cited

Allegheny County Sanitary Authority, 2008, Wet Weather Improvement Program quality assurance project plan report 2006–2008 field program: Allegheny County Sanitary Authority, 70 p.

Alley, E.R., 2000, Water quality control handbook: New York, McGraw-Hill, Inc., p. 1.1–13.11 + 18 appendices.

Barans, C.A., and Tubb, R.A., 1973, Temperatures selected seasonally by four fishes from western Lake Erie: Journal of the Fisheries Research Board of Canada, v. 30, p. 1697–1703.

Beitinger, T.L., Bennett, W.A., and McCauley, R.W., 2000, Temperature tolerances of North American freshwater fishes exposed to dynamic changes in temperature: Environmental Biology of Fishes, v. 58, p. 237–275.

Biggs, B.J.F., 2000, Eutrophication of streams and rivers— Dissolved nutrient-chlorophyll relationships for benthic algae: Journal North American Benthological Society, v. 19, no. 1, p. 17–31.

Blazer, V., Iwanowicz, D., and Iwanowicz, L., 2006, Evaluation of fish health at selected sites in the Shenandoah and comparison with sites in other drainages, *in* Kain, D., and Reeser, S., Shenandoah River fish kills investigations status report, 2006:   Virginia Department of Environmental Quality and Virginia Department of Game and Inland Fisheries.

Blazer, V., Iwanowicz, D., Iwanowicz, L., and Crawford, K., 2009, Intersex and other reproductive abnormalities in fishes from rivers in Pennsylvania [abs.]:   Lancaster, Pa., 65th Annual Northeast Fish and Wildlife Conference, April 26–28, 2009.

Canadian Council of Ministers of the Environment, 1999, Canadian water-quality guidelines for the protection of aquatic life—Dissolved oxygen (freshwater):   Canadian Environmental Quality Guidelines, Winnipeg, 6 p.

Chetelat, J., Pick, F.R., Morin, A., and Hamilton, P.B., 1999, Periphyton biomass and community composition in rivers of different nutrient status: Canadian Journal of Fisheries and Aquatic Sciences, v. 56, no. 4, p. 560–569.

Cohen, S., Lubow, S., and Pflaumer, J., 2009, New Jersey nutrient criteria enhancement plan: New Jersey Department of Environmental Protection, Water Monitoring and Standards, 29 p.

Commission for Environmental Cooperation, 1997, Ecological regions of North America—Toward a common perspective: Communications and Public Outreach Department of the CEC Secretariat, 71 p.

Cooper, E.L., and Wagner, C.C., 1973, The effects of acid mine drainage on fish populations, *in* Pickering, Q.H., project manager, Fish and food organisms in acid mine waters of Pennsylvania: Washington, D.C., U.S. Environmental Protection Agency, p. 75–123

Cuff, D.J., Young, W.J., Muller, E.K., Zelinsky, W., and Abler, R.F., eds., 1989, The atlas of Pennsylvania: Philadelphia, Temple University Press, p. 18–25.

Dauwalter, D.C., and Fisher, W.L., 2007, Spawning chronology, nest site selection, and nest success of smallmouth bass during benign streamflow conditions: The American Midland Naturalist, v. 158, p. 60–78.

Decostere, A., Haesebrouck, F., Turnbull, J.F., and Charlier, G., 1999, Influence of water quality and temperature on adhesion of high and low virulence *Flavobacterium columnare* strains to isolated gill arches: Journal of Fish Diseases, v. 22, p. 1–11.

Dodds, W.K., Jones, J.R., and Welch, E.B., 1998, Suggested classification of stream trophic state—Distributions of temperate stream types by chlorophyll, total nitrogen, and phosphorus: Water Research, v. 32, no. 5, p. 1455–1462.

Dodds, W.K., Smith, V.H., and Lohman, Kirk, 2002, Nitrogen and phosphorus relationships to benthic algal biomass in temperate streams: Canadian Journal of Fisheries and Aquatic Sciences, v. 59, p. 865–874.

Dodds, W.K., Smith, V.H., and Zander, B., 1997, Developing nutrient targets to control benthic chlorophyll levels in stream—A cast study of the Clark Fork River: Water Resources Bulletin, v. 31, p. 1738–1750.

Dodds, W.K., and Welch, E.B., 2000, Establishing nutrient criteria in streams: Journal of North American Benthological Society, v. 19, no. 1, p. 186–196.

Durborow, R.M., Thune, R.L., Hawke, J.P., and Camus, A.C., 1998, Columnaris disease—A bacterial infection caused by *Flavobacterium columnare*: Southern Regional Aquaculture Center, publication number 479, 4 p.

Eagle Valley Environmental Program, 2005, Quality assurance project plan for monitoring of surface water, Eagle Valley Reservation: Eagle Valley Band of Indians, Shasta County, California, 84 p.

Edwards, E.A., Gebhart, G., and Maughan, O.E., 1983, Habitat suitability information—Smallmouth bass: U.S. Department of Interior, Fish and Wildlife Service, FWS/OBS-82/10.36, 47 p.

Garman, Greg, and Orth, Donald, 2007, Fish kills in the Shenandoah River Basin—Preliminary report of the Shenandoah River Basin Science Team: Virginia Department of Environmental Quality, Va., 16 p.

Glassmeyer, S.T., 2007, The cycle of emerging contaminants: Water Resources Impact, v. 9, no. 3, p. 5–7.

Helsel, D.R., and Hirsch, R.M., 2002, Statistical methods in water resources: U.S. Geological Survey Techniques of Water-Resources Investigations, book 4, chap. A3, p. 118–124 and 142–147.

Hem, J.D., 1985, Study and interpretation of the chemical characteristics of natural water (3d ed.): U.S. Geological Survey Water-Supply Paper 2254, 263 p.

Hill, Jennifer, 1989, Analysis of six foraging behaviors as toxicity indicators, using juvenile smallmouth bass exposed to low environmental pH: Archives of Environmental Contamination and Toxicology, v. 18, p. 895–899.

Hill, Jennifer, Foley, R.E., Blazer, V.S., Werner, R.G., and Gannon, J.E., 1988, Effects of acidic water on young-of-the-year smallmouth bass (*Micropterus dolomieui*): Environmental Biology of Fishes, v. 21, p. 223–229.

Langland, M.J., Bloomquist, J.D., and Hyer, K.E., 2009, Summary of results for the 2008 Chesapeake Bay Nontidal Trends Network: accessed September 4, 2009, at *http://va.water.usgs.gov/chesbay/RIMP/2008trends.html*

Langland, M.J., Raffensperger, J.P., Moyer, D.L., Landwehr, J.M., and Schwartz, G.E., 2006, Changes in streamflow and water quality in selected nontidal basins in the Chesapeake Bay Watershed, 1985–2004: U.S. Geological Survey Scientific Investigations Report 2006-5178, 75 p.

Lohman, K., Jones, J.R., and Perkins, B.D., 1992, Effects of nutrient enrichment and flood frequency on periphyton biomass in northern Ozark streams: Canadian Journal of Fisheries and Aquatic Sciences, v. 49, p. 1198–1205.

Lombard, S.M., and Kirchmer, C.J., 2004, Guidelines for preparing quality assurance project plans for environmental studies: Washington State Department of Ecology Publication No. 04-03-030, 82 p.

Maule, A.G., and Schreck, C.B., 1990, Changes in number of leukocytes in immune organs of juvenile coho salmon (*Oncorhynchus kisutch*) after acute stress or cortisol treatment: Journal of Aquatic Animal Health, v. 2, p. 298–304.

McGonigal, K.H., 2008, Nutrients and suspended sediment transported in the Susquehanna River Basin, 2007, and trends, January 1985 through December 2007: Susquehanna River Basin Commission Publication No 262, 30 p.

New Jersey Office of Information Technology, 2009, New Jersey 2007-2008 High Resolution Orthophotography, MrSID 5K Tiles: accessed July 29, 2009, at *https://njgin.state.nj.us/NJ_NJGINExplorer/DataDownloads.jsp*

Nimick, D.A., Cleasby, T.E., and McCleskey, R.B., 2005, Seasonality of diel cycles of dissolved metal concentrations in a Rocky Mountain stream: Environmental Geology, v. 47, p. 603–614.

Noga, E.J., 1988, Determining the relationship between water quality and infectious disease in fishery populations: American Water Resources Association, v. 24, p. 967–973.

Pennsylvania Department of Conservation and Natural Resources, 2000, Physiographic provinces of Pennsylvania (4th ed.) [online]: Bureau of Topographic and Geologic Survey, map 13, accessed July 8, 2009, at *http://www.dcnr.state.pa.us/topogeo/map13/amp13.aspx*

Pennsylvania Department of Environmental Protection, 2009a, Pennsylvania code, Title 25, § 93.7: accessed August 17, 2009, at *http://www/pacode.com/secure/data/025/chapter93/s93.7.html*

Pennsylvania Department of Environmental Protection, 2009b, Facilities in Pa. with an NPDES Permit: Wastewater Information Page, accessed on July 13, 2009, at *http://www.depweb.state.pa.us/watersupply/lib/watersupply/NPDESPermits_PM2009.xls*

Pennsylvania Fish and Boat Commission, 2005, As research continues into causes and effects of smallmouth bass die-off, young of the year analysis provides encouraging news: accessed July 10, 2009, at *http://www.fish.state.pa.us/newsreleases/2005/smb_yoy.htm*

Pennsylvania Fish and Boat Commission, 2009, Pennsylvania Fishes: accessed August 17, 2009, at *http://www.fish.state.pa.us/pafish/fishhtms/chapindx.htm*

Pennsylvania Spatial Data Access, 2009, Enhanced PASDA service: The Pennsylvania imagery navigator, accessed July 29, 2009, at *http://www.pasda.psu.edu/*.

Ponader, K.C., Charles, D.F., and Belton, T.J., 2007, Diatom–based TP and TN models and indices for monitoring nutrient enrichment of New Jersey streams: Ecological Indicators, v. 7, p. 79–93.

Potapova, Marina, and Charles, D.F., 2007, Diatom metrics for monitoring eutrophication in rivers of the United States: Ecological Indicators, v. 7, p. 48–70.

Ridgway, M.S., Gogg, G.P., and Keenleyside, M.H.A., 1989, Courtship and spawning behavior in smallmouth bass (*Micropterus dolomieui*): The American Midland Naturalist, v. 122, p. 209–213.

Ripley, J., Iwanowicz, L., Blazer, V., and Foran, C., 2008, Utilization of protein expression profiles as indicators of environmental impairment of smallmouth bass (*Micropterus dolomieui*) from the Shenandoah River, Virginia, USA: Environmental Toxicology and Chemistry, v. 27, no. 8, p. 1756–1767.

Risser, D.W., and Siwiec, S.F., 1996, Water-quality assessment of the lower Susquehanna River Basin, Pennsylvania and Maryland—Environmental setting: U.S. Geological Survey Water-Resources Investigations Report 94-4245, 70 p.

Robertson, L.S., Iwanowicz, L.R., and Marranca, J.M., 2009, Identification of centrarchid hepcidins and evidence that 17β-estradiol disrupts constitutive expression of hepcidin-1 and inducible expression of hepcidin-2 in largemouth bass (*Micropterus salmoides*): Fish and Shellfish Immunology, v. 26, p. 898–907.

Salvato, J.A., 1992, Environmental engineering and sanitation (4th ed.): New York, John Wiley & Sons, Inc., 1418 p.

Sawyer, C.N., McCarty, P.L., and Parkin, G.F., 2003, Chemistry for environmental engineering and science (5th ed.): New York, McGraw-Hill, 752 p.

Scholefield, David, Goff, T.L., Braven, Jim, Ebdon, Les, Long, Terry, and Butler, Mark, 2005, Concerted diurnal patterns in riverine nutrient concentrations and physical conditions: Science of the Total Environment, v. 344, p. 201–210.

Schreer, J.F., and Cooke, S.J., 2002, Behavioral and physiological responses of smallmouth bass to a dynamic thermal environment: American Fisheries Society Symposium, v. 31, p. 191–203.

Scott, D.M., Lucas, M.C., and Wilson, R.W., 2005, The effect of high pH on ion balance, nitrogen excretion, and behavior in freshwater fish from an eutrophic lake—A laboratory and field study: Aquatic Toxicology, v. 73, p. 31–43.

Sheeder, S.A., and Evans, B.M., 2004, Estimating nutrient and sediment threshold criteria for biological impairment in Pennsylvania watersheds: Journal of the American Water Resources Association, v. 40, p. 881–888.

Siefert, R.E., Carlson, A.R., and Herman, L.J., 1974, Effects of reduced oxygen concentrations on the early life stages of mountain whitefish, smallmouth bass, and white bass: The Progressive Fish-Culturist, v. 36, no. 4, p. 186–190.

Spoor, W.A., 1984, Oxygen requirements of the smallmouth bass, *Micropterus dolomieui* Lacépède: Journal of Fisheries Biology, v. 25, p. 587–592.

Stevenson, R.J., Rier, S.T., Riseng, C.M., Schultz, R.E., and Wiley, M.J., 2006, Comparing effects of nutrients on algal biomass in streams in two regions with different disturbance regimes and with applications for developing nutrient criteria: Hydrobiologia, v. 561, p. 149–165.

Suomalainen, L-R., Tiirola, M.A., and Valtonen, E.T., 2005, Influence of rearing conditions on Flavobacterium columnare infection of rainbow trout, Oncorhynchus mykiss (Walbaum): Journal of Fish Diseases, v. 28, p. 271–277.

U.S. Army Corps of Engineers, 2004, C.W. Bill Young Lock and Dam, U.S. Army Corps of Engineers Allegheny River Chart No. 5: accessed April 8, 2009, at *http://www.lrp.usace.army.mil/nav/ nav.htm#_Allegheny_River_Navigation_Charts*

U.S. Environmental Protection Agency, 1986, Ambient water quality criteria for dissolved oxygen: EPA Number 440586003, 62 p.

U.S. Environmental Protection Agency, 1993, Methods for the determination of inorganic substances in environmental samples: U.S. Environmental Protection Agency report number EPA/600/R-93/100, Washington, D.C.

U.S. Environmental Protection Agency, 2002, Summary table for the nutrient criteria documents: accessed April 14, 2009, at *http://www.epa.gov/waterscience/criteria/nutrient/ ecoregions/index.html*

U.S. Environmental Protection Agency, 2008, State adoption of nutrient standards (1998-2008): U.S. Environmental Protection Agency, Office of Water, EPA-821-F-08-007, 12 p. + appendices.

U.S. Environmental Protection Agency, 2009, Quality Assurance Planning: U.S. Environmental Protection Agency, Region 9, accessed September 10, 2009, at *http://www.epa.gov/region09/qa/projplans.html*

U.S. Geological Survey, 2003, User's manual for the National Water Information System of the U.S. Geological Survey automated data processing system (ADAPS): U.S. Geological Survey Open-File Report 03-123, version 4.3, 407 p.

Vollenweider, R.A., 1968, Scientific fundamentals of the eutrophication of lakes and flowing waters, with particular reference to nitrogen and phosphorus as factors in eutrophication: Paris, Organisation for Economic Co-operation and Development, Technical Report DAS/SCI/68.27, 250 p.

Wang, W.B., Li, A.H., Cai, T.Z., and Wang, J.G., 2005, Effects of intraperitoneal injection of cortisol on nonspecific immune functions of Ctenopharyngodon idella: Journal of Fish Biology, v. 67, p. 779–793.

Wagner, R.J., Boulger, Jr., R.W., Oblinger, C.J., and Smith, B.A., 2006, Guidelines and standard procedures for continuous water-quality monitors—Station operation, record computation, and data reporting: U.S. Geological Survey Techniques and Methods I-D3, 51 p. plus attachments.

Webb, B.W., and Noblis, Franz, 2007, Long-term changes in river temperature and the influence of climatic and hydrological factors: Hydrological Sciences, v. 52, no. 1, p. 74–85.

Welker, T.L., McNulty, S.T., and Klesius, P.H., 2007, Effect of sub lethal hypoxia on the immune response and susceptibility of channel catfish, *Ictalurus punctatus*, to enteric septicemia: Journal of the World Aquaculture Society, v. 38, no. 1, p. 12–22.

Whitmore, T.J., 1989, Florida diatom assemblages as indicators of trophic state and pH: Limnology and Oceanography, v. 34, no. 5, p. 882–895.

Wilde, R.D., Radtke, D.B., Gibs, J., and Iwatsubo, R.T., 1998, National field manual for the collection of water-quality data: U.S. Geological Survey Techniques of Water-Resources Investigations, book 9, variously paged.

Yellow Springs Instruments, 1999, Environmental monitoring systems operations manual: Yellow Springs, Ohio, 264 p.

Appendix 1.   Quality Control

Summary of results for quality-control samples and results for nutrients in water and streambed sediment, 2008.

Medium	Type of quality-control sample	Number of samples submitted	Number of constituents exceeding data-quality objective
Water	Field blank sample	6	0 out of 42 analyzed
	Duplicate sample	4	1 out of 28 analyzed
	Reference water sample	1	1 out of 7 analyzed
Bottom sediment	Duplicate sample	5	2 out of 15 analyzed

Appendix 2.   Selected Statistics for Dissolved-Oxygen Concentrations

Values for 7-day mean minimum and 7-day mean dissolved-oxygen concentrations at selected stations in Pennsylvania and New Jersey, May 1 through July 31, 2008.

[C1, Delaware River at Trenton, N.J.; C2, Susquehanna River at Shady Nook Boat Launch; C3, Susquehanna River below Clemson Island (Main Channel); C4, Susquehanna River at Clemson Island (Microhabitat); C5, Juniata River at Newport, Pa.; C6, Juniata River near Howe Township Park (Microhabitat); C7, Juniata River near Howe Township Park (Main Channel); C8, Susquehanna River at Harrisburg, Pa.; C10, Allegheny River at Lock and Dam 3 at Acmetonia, Pa.; mg/L, milligrams per liter; n, number of 7-day mean minimum or 7-day mean values; P25, 25th percentile; P75, 75th percentile; —, not computed]

| Statistic | 7-Day mean minimum dissolved oxygen (mg/L) | | | | | | | | |
| | Station | | | | | | | | |
	C1	C2	C3	C4	C5	C6	C7	C8	C10
n	69	—	70	70	56	53	51	67	73
Minimum	6.0	—	5.4	3.8	4.8	4.6	5.1	5.0	6.0
P25	7.4	—	6.0	4.9	5.8	5.2	5.7	5.9	6.5
Median	7.8	—	6.3	5.3	6.0	5.4	6.0	6.0	7.0
P75	8.6	—	6.9	5.6	6.4	5.6	6.2	6.3	9.0
Maximum	9.7	—	10.0	9.7	9.7	6.6	7.0	9.6	9.4
Mean	7.9	—	6.7	5.6	6.3	5.4	6.0	6.3	7.6
Standard deviation	1.0	—	1.2	1.3	1.0	.5	.5	1.0	1.2

| Statistic | 7-Day mean dissolved oxygen (mg/L) | | | | | | | | |
| | Station | | | | | | | | |
	C1	C2	C3	C4	C5	C6	C7	C8	C10
n	69	—	70	70	56	53	51	67	73
Minimum	6.8	—	7.8	6.2	7.8	6.9	7.8	6.6	6.6
P25	9.0	—	8.1	7.0	8.1	7.4	8.3	7.1	7.0
Median	9.3	—	8.2	7.3	8.3	7.6	8.6	7.2	7.3
P75	9.7	—	8.7	7.6	8.9	7.8	8.8	7.8	9.2
Maximum	10.7	—	10.5	10.1	10.0	8.8	9.8	9.8	9.5
Mean	9.1	—	8.5	7.5	8.5	7.6	8.6	7.5	7.9
Standard deviation	.9	—	.7	.9	.6	.4	.5	.7	1.1

Appendix 3.   Nutrient Concentrations in Water and Streambed Sediment

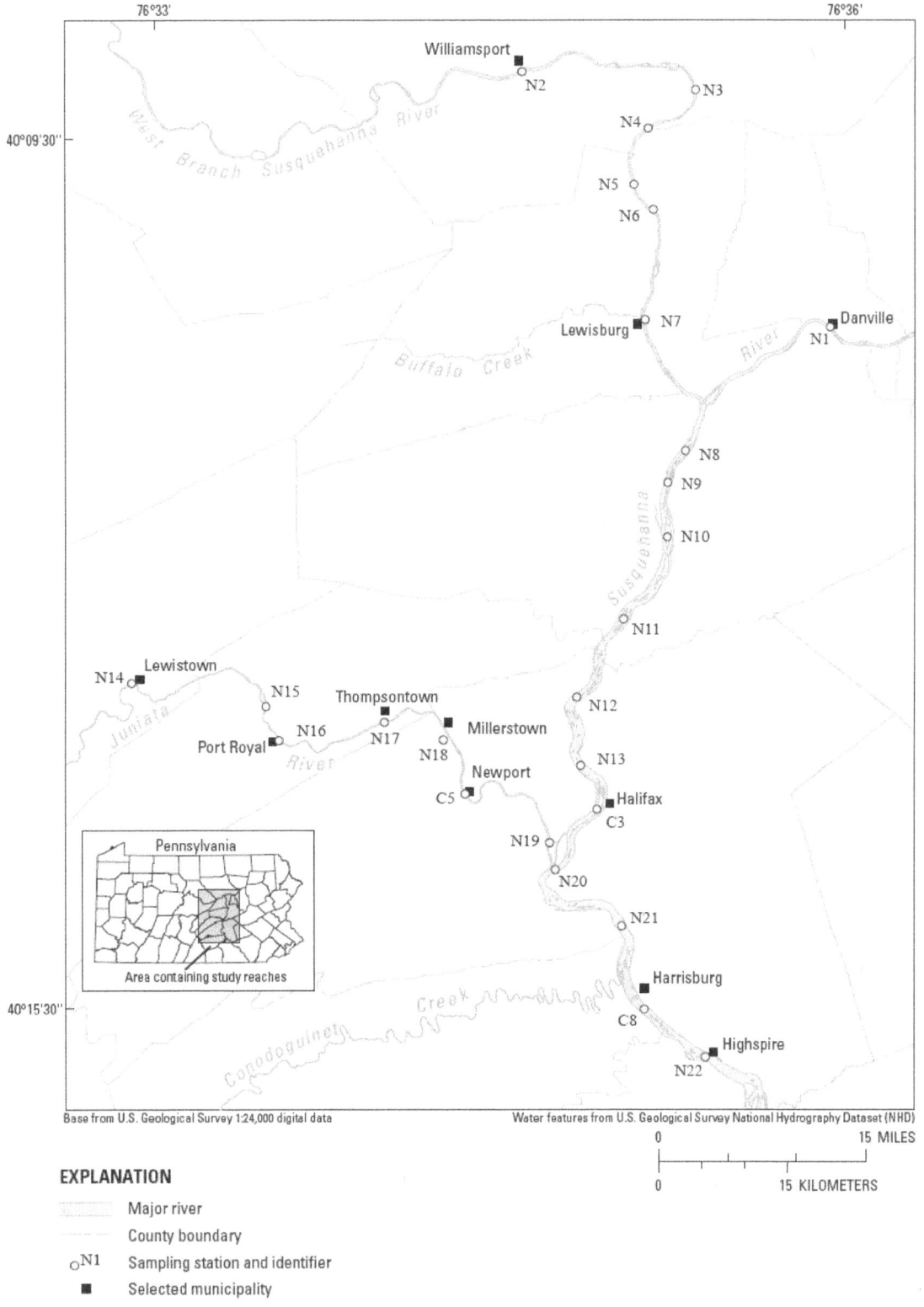

Figure 3-1.   Locations of stations selected for the nutrient synoptic survey in the Susquehanna River Basin, Pennsylvania, June 11 and 12, 2008.

Table 3-1. Concentrations of nitrogen and phosphorus species from water and streambed-sediment samples collected from the West Branch Susquehanna River, June 11 and 12, 2008.

[mg/L, milligrams per liter; g/kg, grams per kilogram; <, less than]

Station name	Map identifier	Water							Streambed sediment		
		Ammonia plus organic nitrogen as nitrogen (mg/L)	Ammonia as nitrogen (mg/L)	Nitrate as nitrogen (mg/L)	Nitrite as nitrogen (mg/L)	Total nitrogen (mg/L)	Ortho-phosphate as phosphate (mg/L)	Phosphorus as phosphorus (mg/L)	Ammonia plus organic nitrogen as nitrogen (g/kg)	Total ammonia as nitrogen (g/kg)	Total phosphorus as phosphorus (g/kg)
West Branch Susquehanna River at											
Duboistown, Pa. (right bank)	N2	<1	0.03	0.45	<0.01	0.75	<0.01	0.034	1.161	0.01	0.5
Duboistown, Pa. (left bank)	N2	<1	<.02	.41	<.01	.7	<.01	.011	1.798	.02	.54
Muncy, Pa. (right bank)	N3	<1	<.05	.59	<.01	.78	<.01	.014	.606	.01	.25
Muncy, Pa. (left bank)	N3	<1	<.05	.75	<.01	.99	<.01	.018	.302	.01	.1
Montgomery, Pa. (right bank)	N4	<1	.02	.51	<.01	.72	<.01	.011	.28	<.01	.2
Montgomery, Pa. (left bank)	N4	<1	.02	.5	<.01	.71	<.01	.013	1.207	.01	.4
Allenwood, Pa. (right bank)	N5	<1	<.05	.56	.01	.81	<.01	.015	.509	.01	.24
Allenwood, Pa. (left bank)	N5	<1	<.05	.5	<.01	.74	<.01	.016	.767	.01	.33
Watsontown, Pa. (right bank)	N6	<1	<.05	.56	<.01	.8	<.01	.021	.996	.01	.34
Watsontown, Pa. (left bank)	N6	<1	<.05	.53	<.01	.77	<.01	.015	.231	<.01	.15
Lewisburg, Pa. (right bank)	N7	<1	.03	1.54	.02	1.85	.035	.061	.665	.01	.24
Lewisburg, Pa. (left bank)	N7	<1	.02	.74	<.01	.98	<.01	.016	.364	<.01	.21

Table 3-2. Concentrations of nitrogen and phosphorus species from water and streambed-sediment samples collected from the Juniata River, June 11 and 12, 2008.

[mg/L, milligrams per liter; g/kg, grams per kilogram; <, less than]

Station name	Map identifier	Water							Streambed sediment		
		Ammonia plus organic nitrogen as nitrogen (mg/L)	Ammonia as nitrogen (mg/L)	Nitrate as nitrogen (mg/L)	Nitrite as nitrogen (mg/L)	Total nitrogen (mg/L)	Ortho-phosphate as phosphate (mg/L)	Phosphorus as phosphorus (mg/L)	Ammonia plus organic nitrogen as nitrogen (g/kg)	Total ammonia as nitrogen (g/kg)	Total phosphorus as phosphorus (g/kg)
Juniata River at											
Lewistown, Pa. (right bank)	N14	<1	<0.1	1.23	<0.04	1.56	0.022	0.037	1.583	0.02	0.4
Lewistown, Pa. (left bank)	N14	<1	.11	1.22	<.04	1.59	.026	.044	1.983	.04	.91
Mifflintown, Pa. (right bank)	N15	<1	<.1	1.42	<.04	1.72	.023	.043	.43	.01	.35
Mifflintown, Pa. (left bank)	N15	<1	.11	1.41	<.04	1.72	.027	.044	2.639	.05	.83
Port Royal, Pa. (right bank)	N16	<1	<.05	1.25	.02	1.7	.019	.042	2.747	.05	.95
Port Royal, Pa. (left bank)	N16	<1	<.05	1.32	.02	1.8	.019	.048	2.294	.01	.26
Thompsontown, Pa. (right bank)	N17	<1	.05	1.19	.01	1.67	.017	.04	.606	.01	.26
Thompsontown, Pa. (left bank)	N17	<1	.05	1.32	.02	1.79	.017	.041	.844	.01	.28
Millerstown, Pa. (right bank)	N18	<1	.05	1.15	.01	1.6	.017	.03	2.14	.03	.6
Millerstown, Pa. (left bank)	N18	<1	<.05	1.38	.02	1.84	.021	.043	1.491	.02	.47
Newport, Pa. (right bank)	C5	<1	<.05	1.12	.01	1.54	.014	.039	1.043	.03	.25
Newport, Pa. (left bank)	C5	<1	<.05	1.28	.02	1.78	.02	.042	1.69	.04	.54
Amity Hall, Pa. (right bank)	N19	<1	<.05	1.06	.02	1.46	.013	.033	3.63	.08	.99
Amity Hall, Pa. (left bank)	N19	<1	<.05	1.2	.02	1.62	.017	.041	2.676	.06	.69

Table 3-3. Concentrations of nitrogen and phosphorus species from water and streambed-sediment samples collected from the mainstem Susquehanna River, June 11 and 12, 2008.

[mg/L, milligrams per liter; g/kg, grams per kilogram; <, less than; na, no sample collected]

Station name	Map identifier	Water							Streambed sediment		
		Ammonia plus organic nitrogen as nitrogen (mg/L)	Ammonia as nitrogen (mg/L)	Nitrate as nitrogen (mg/L)	Nitrite as nitrogen (mg/L)	Total nitrogen (mg/L)	Ortho-phosphate as phosphate (mg/L)	Phosphorus as phosphorus (mg/L)	Ammonia plus organic nitrogen as nitrogen (g/kg)	Total ammonia as nitrogen (g/kg)	Total phosphorus as phosphorus (g/kg)
Right bank—Susquehanna River											
at Danville, Pa.	N1	<1	0.02	0.29	<0.04	0.84	<0.01	0.05	1.101	0.02	0.36
at Sunbury, Pa.	N8	<1	<.05	.18	<.01	.78	<.01	.018	1.702	.01	.52
near Fishers Island at Selinsgrove, Pa.	N9	<1	<.05	.48	<.01	.7	<.01	.017	1.114	.01	.44
at Hoover Island	N10	<1	<.05	.48	<.01	.79	<.01	.017	1.122	<.01	.37
at Dalmatia, Pa.	N11	<1	<.1	.92	<.04	1.18	.013	.039	2.02	.02	.46
at Liverpool, Pa.	N12	<1	<.1	.72	<.04	.99	<.01	.024	1.027	.01	.33
at Montgomery Ferry, Pa.	N13	<1	<.1	.6	<.04	.88	<.01	.02	1.271	.02	.29
below Clemson Island	C3	<1	<.02	.65	<.04	.88	<.01	.024	1.244	<.01	.27
near Duncannon, Pa.	N20	<1	<.1	.6	<.04	.86	<.01	.019	1.543	<.01	.28
at Marysville, Pa.	N21	<1	<.1	.97	<.04	1.29	<.01	.027	2.964	.07	.84
at Harrisburg, Pa.	C8	<1	<.1	3.54	<.04	3.77	.016	.03	3.004	.05	1.04
at Highspire, Pa.	N22	<1	.06	.27	.01	.91	<.01	.041	1.733	.02	.56

Table 3-3. Concentrations of nitrogen and phosphorus species from water and streambed-sediment samples collected from the mainstem Susquehanna River, June 11 and 12, 2008.—Continued

[mg/L, milligrams per liter; g/kg, grams per kilogram; <, less than; na, no sample collected]

Station name	Map identifier	Water							Streambed sediment		
		Ammonia plus organic nitrogen as nitrogen (mg/L)	Ammonia as nitrogen (mg/L)	Nitrate as nitrogen (mg/L)	Nitrite as nitrogen (mg/L)	Total nitrogen (mg/L)	Ortho-phosphate as phosphorus (mg/L)	Phosphorus as phosphorus (mg/L)	Ammonia plus organic nitrogen as nitrogen (g/kg)	Total ammonia as nitrogen (g/kg)	Total phosphorus as phosphorus (g/kg)
Left bank—Susquehanna River											
at Danville, Pa.	N1	<1	<0.02	0.37	<0.04	0.9	<0.01	0.037	0.878	0.02	0.35
at Sunbury, Pa.	N8	<1	<.05	.18	<.01	.78	<.01	.033	2.223	.01	.55
near Fishers Island at Selinsgrove, Pa.	N9	<1	<.1	.29	<.04	.76	<.01	.025	1.201	<.01	.53
at Hoover Island	N10	<1	<.05	.31	<.01	.82	<.01	.035	1.862	.02	.69
at Dalmatia, Pa.	N11	<1	<.05	.42	<.01	.88	<.01	.029	3.955	.04	.94
at Liverpool, Pa.	N12	<1	<.05	.5	<.01	.98	<.01	.028	3.16	.04	1.43
at Montgomery Ferry, Pa.	N13	<1	<.05	.66	<.01	1.14	<.01	.051	.413	<.01	.17
below Clemson Island	C3	<1	<.05	.45	<.01	1.02	<.01	.038	2.312	.04	.65
near Duncannon, Pa.	N20	<1	.03	.55	<.01	1.01	<.01	.04	2.134	.03	.73
at Marysville, Pa.	N21	<1	.03	.23	<.01	.72	<.01	.027	1.184	.03	.37
at Harrisburg, Pa.	C8	<1	.04	.21	<.01	.74	<.01	.032	na	na	na
at Highspire, Pa.	N22	<1	.1	2.08	<.04	2.37	.028	.047	2.473	.04	.73

USGS

Chaplin and others—Water-Quality Monitoring in Response to Young-of-the-Year Smallmouth Bass Mortality, Pennsylvania—OFR 2009-1216